Dedication

Thanks to all those who have contributed to my adventures over the past 45 years. I have enjoyed the trips and the companionship immensely. The photos they have posed for and taken are an important part of this book. This book comes from those people as well as from me.

I must again thank my high school English teacher, Joan L. Baxter. My success is a reflection on her guidance through my high school years.

ALASKA WEAR
THE VISITOR'S GUIDE TO CLOTHING & GEAR

by Tony Russ

Northern Publishing
Wasilla, Alaska

ALASKA WEAR
THE VISITOR'S GUIDE TO CLOTHING & GEAR
by Tony Russ

Copyright © 2001 by Tony R. Russ

All rights reserved. No part of this book may be reproduced or transmitted in any form or by any means, electronic or mechanical, including photocopying, without prior written permission of the Publisher, except in the case of brief quotations as part of critical reviews, newspapers, magazines, newsletters and catalogs.

Wraparound Cover Photo: Barry Arm in Prince William Sound, by AlaskaPhotoGraphics.com, Patrick J. Endres, P.O. Box 81312, Fairbanks, Alaska 99708, www.alaskaphotographics.com

Back Cover Inset Photo: Coxe glacier in Prince William Sound by Author; vessel is the Discovery –berthed in Whittier, Alaska: Discovery Voyages, P.O. Box 688, Whittier, Alaska 99693, 1-800-324-7602, www.discoveryvoyages.com

Editor: Diane O'Loughlin
Illustrator: Cynthia Cassell

First Edition, April 2001
Produced in Alaska
Printed in the United States of America

Published by:
Northern Publishing
P.O. Box 871803
Wasilla, Alaska 99687-1803
E-mail: northernp@ak.net
http://home.gci.net/~northernpublishing (our web address may change–do a search for "Northern Publishing" to find us)

CONTENTS

TABLE OF CONTENTS
ABOUT THE AUTHOR
INTRODUCTION
CHAPTER ONE – **OVERVIEW OF ALASKA'S CLIMATE** 11
    Generalizations about Climate and Weather, Temperature and Precipitation Maps, Average Temperatures, Average Snowfall, Total Precipitation, Statewide Summary
CHAPTER TWO – **ALASKAN DESTINATIONS** 25
    Arctic, Interior, Western/Bering Sea Coast, Southwestern/Alaska Peninsula, Southcentral/Gulf Coast, Southeast; **CITIES' CLIMATE DESCRIPTIONS,** Normal Maximum/Minimum Temperature, Precipitation Days & Total Precipitation, Monthly Snowfall, Humidity, Average Wind Speed, Daylight on 15th, Aurora Index, Bug index; **CITIES' CLIMATE TABLES**
CHAPTER THREE – **CLOTHING SELECTION GUIDELINES** 79
    Heat Transfer & Retention, Hypothermia, Clothing Features, Fabrics, Waterproof Fabrics, Layering, Clothing Selection
CHAPTER FOUR – **FOOTWEAR EVALUATION** 101
    Selection of Footwear, The Right Fit, Break-in Process Waterproofing, Field Care of Footwear, Socks, An Effective Sock Strategy, Foot Medicine
CHAPTER FIVE – **PHOTOGRAPHY, CAMERAS & BINOCULARS** 111
    Subjects to Photograph, Composition, Traveling Cameras and Film, Binoculars
CHAPTER SIX – **LUGGAGE STRATEGY FOR ALASKA** 121
    Hard-sided Luggage, Soft Duffel
CHAPTER SEVEN – **GEARING UP FOR ALASKAN CAMPING** 125
    Tough Fabrics for Gear, Tents, Sleeping Bags, Pads & Cots, Stoves & Cooking Gear, Map & Compass, Packs, Miscellaneous Gear, Backpackers' Check List
CHAPTER EIGHT – **FIREARMS/PROTECTION FOR VISITORS** 155
    Bears, Wolves & Other Canines, In General, Firearms

CONTENTS

CHAPTER NINE **– WATER QUALITY & FIRST AID** 161
   Our Water Needs, Water Quality, First Aid
CHAPTER TEN **– CLOTHING AND GEAR RECOMMENDATIONS
            FOR ALASKAN DESTINATIONS** 171
   Base Layer, Second/Insulating Layer, Protective/Outer Layer, Footwear, Luggage and Duffel, Camping/Backpacking and Miscellaneous Gear, **SOURCES OF CLOTHING AND GEAR**
CONCLUSION 191
   INDEX
   BIBLIOGRAPHY
   ALASKAN ART
   BOOK ORDER FORM

ABOUT THE AUTHOR

Tony Russ was born in Anchorage, Alaska, when it was still a Territory of the U.S. Alaska became our 49th state in 1959. Tony grew up in Alaska enjoying all the outdoor activities which now attract over one million visitors per year. He has traveled to hundreds of Alaska's more remote destinations for work or play–often for both.

During his 45 years in Alaska, Tony has been employed as a Construction Worker, State Fish & Game Biologist, Oil Field Geochemist, and Science Teacher. He has been self-employed as a Taxi Driver, Window Washer, Ice Cream Parlor Owner, Hunting Guide, Artist, Writer and Publisher. He currently makes his living by guiding, writing, publishing and creating art–all four pursuits based on the Alaskan outdoors.

Tony's first book was self-published in 1994. Since then he has written three more–counting this one. His books are successful because of his ability to research a subject, analyze it, and then present it in an organized form which readers can easily understand. Feedback from readers has helped him improve his writing as well as direct him toward future topics. Please feel free to send comments about this or any of his books via any communication method listed on the copyright page.

INTRODUCTION

- Winds over 130 mph
- Annual snowfall over 974 inches
- Highest recorded snowpack in North America of 356 inches
- Mountain ranges over 20,000 ft.
- Highest pressure reading in North America - 31.85 inches
- North America's strongest earthquake - 9.2 on Richter scale
- Ambient temperature of -80° F
- Ambient temperature of 100° F
- Aurora Borealis visible from Fairbanks about 240 days per year

WHAT THIS BOOK WILL DO FOR YOU

Alaska's state motto is "The Last Frontier." As such it carries with it an aura of the unknown–a destination with a little mystery surrounding it. In fact, there are a lot of unknowns as well as many outright misconceptions about Alaska. Some of those misconceptions involve the climate (average weather conditions) of Alaska. **All of the climate extremes (and the other natural occurrences) listed above are actually true facts about Alaska.** But, taken by themselves these climate extremes do not give a clear picture of what **weather** you might expect during a short visit to Alaska.

This book will clear up the unknowns and dispel the misconceptions about the climate of "The Last Frontier." This will be accomplished by giving you information about statewide climate over the past 30-50 years. In just a few short minutes of casual observation, the temperature and precipitation maps in Chapter One will show you the normal temperatures and precipitation levels for every month of the year in all areas of Alaska.

Then, in Chapter Two, you can choose cities from all over the state and see specifics about their climate. You will be able to determine when the driest month is for a Southeast destination or when the warmest month is for a city on the Arctic coast. You can also find out when the best time is to see the Aurora Borealis and which region has the best viewing opportunities.

Next, I will give you detailed information about how clothing, footwear and gear perform their functions from a technical standpoint. Whether you are going on an all-inclusive cruise ship to Southeast or planning a solo trek through the Brooks Range, you will learn how to evaluate the gear you need. The different methods of heat transfer and the qualities of specific outdoor fabrics are two of the topics I will analyze in detail.

Finally, I will give you a list of specific items of name-brand clothing, footwear, gear, luggage, etc. and the uses they are best suited for in Alaska. If your trip to Alaska is the first of many travel adventures and you need to start an extensive outdoor wardrobe, or if your trip is possibly a once-in-a-lifetime adventure of an outdoor nature, I will address your clothing needs. Clothing items for a specific type of weather and gear which is useful for a wide variety of weather conditions are both included in my recommendations section. Included in this section are sources for the items described throughout the book.

By following the guidelines in this book you can have confidence you will be warm, dry and comfortable during your visit to Alaska.

Beautiful summer days like this are what we all dream about. It's those other days we need to be prepared for in order to enjoy the total Alaskan experience.

Huge fish, sunny days, family and friends–Alaskan visitors come north each year for these types of adventures in "The Great Land."

CHAPTER ONE

OVERVIEW OF ALASKA'S CLIMATE

This chapter contains statewide climate generalizations plus temperature and precipitation maps for each month of the year. These can be used to quickly obtain an overall understanding of Alaska's climate. Chapter Two will then explore the climate of many cities in detail. Below is a reference map with the most common destinations in Alaska.

GENERALIZATIONS ABOUT CLIMATE AND WEATHER

Alaska is a land of many extremes: extreme tides, extreme heat and cold, heavy snow and ice, high winds, flooding, thunderstorms, lightning, tornados, tsunamis, earthquakes, avalanches and landslides. One reason for the wide variety of climate and weather patterns is the sheer size of Alaska. The illustration below compares the size of Alaska to the United States.

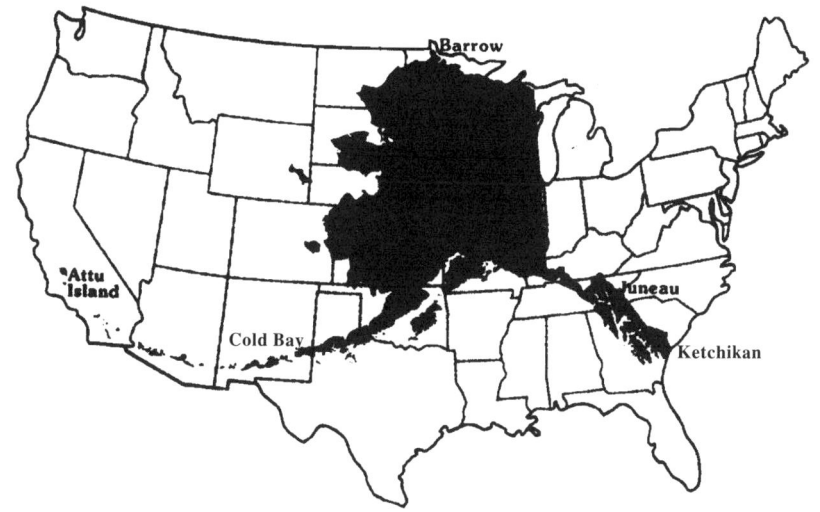

The difference in latitude between Barrow and Ketchikan is as great as the difference between International Falls on the northern Minnesota border and Savannah, Georgia, near the southeast coast of the U.S. The east-west difference for mainland Alaska is similar to that between Savannah and Roswell, New Mexico. It is not surprising that Alaskan weather is hard to predict and dress appropriately for. The state is big, both north to south and east to west. Add to that the vertical difference in Alaskan locations due to the numerous mountain ranges and the result is: on almost any day of the year in Alaska you can encounter warm, summer weather or extreme winter conditions. Therefore, dressing for an Alaskan visit should be taken seriously if you want to be comfortable.

Most Alaskan cities are either on a coastline or next to a river. The difficulty of transportation in this vast state dictated the prudence of these locations. This nearness to water and the associated

Overview of Alaska's Climate 13

moist air and pressure differences equate to a lot of windy, cloudy days and frequent precipitation in most Alaskan cities. Many of Alaska's cities are also found near or in the numerous mountain ranges–another factor which increases wind and precipitation levels.

Because of these wet, windy conditions in Alaska you should always be prepared for at least one season colder than the timing of your visit. A nice spring day can suddenly turn to winter-like weather when clouds appear and a late snowfall dumps six inches of snow on the landscape. In mountainous regions, even during the warmest summer days, a sudden wind coming down off a nearby glacier can create fall weather conditions. Just imagine being next to a large pile of huge ice cubes and suddenly having a large fan turned on, pointing in your direction. Some of this may sound fictional, but it illustrates the type of sudden weather changes you are likely to encounter in Alaska.

Another common experience in Alaska is finding yourself next to a large, cool body of water. Alaska's oceans and rivers contain cold water. Some of the northerly oceans and almost all the rivers statewide are frozen part of the year. In summer the water temperatures don't rise much above freezing and average less than 40° F. Any breeze blowing over them is quickly cooled–even in summer. A comfortable July day in the high 60's can suddenly turn uncomfortably cool if a change in wind direction brings ocean-cooled air inland.

The possibility of sudden, strong breezes bringing cool and possibly wet air from either nearby mountains or cool water bodies should be a major consideration when planning a visit to Alaska. By having some sort of windbreaker handy whenever you are in a coastal region, near a large river or close to a mountain range you can prevent unnecessary discomfort which can make an otherwise great experience a test of your endurance.

Another factor which can suddenly affect your comfort level is Alaska's sun. Because Alaska's climate is cool, the sun has a significant effect on how comfortable we are when outdoors. The earth's atmosphere is thinner over Alaska because of the high latitude. Direct sunshine can therefore have a great affect on how warm you feel. A sunny, 70° F day in Alaska feels much warmer than a

70° day at a lower latitude because Alaska's sun feels hotter. However, if the sun suddenly disappears behind a cloud or goes behind one of the numerous mountains, you will perceive a sudden change in your comfort level. Alaska's hot sun is another reason for wide swings in your comfort level when outdoors and another reason to dress for one season cooler than either the actual or perceived season.

TEMPERATURE AND PRECIPITATION MAPS

There are several crucial points you should remember when looking at the following temperature and precipitation maps of Alaska. First of all, they are very general maps. Since Alaska is a huge state, the temperature lines have, out of necessity, been drawn to include large areas. The local temperature differences caused by topographic barriers which block air movements, elevation changes which average a drop in temperature of three and one-half degrees every thousand feet of elevation and other geographic characteristics cannot be indicated on maps of this scale.

The temperatures are all given in degrees Fahrenheit and are the averages for the entire month, considering the extreme highs and lows. Daily highs and lows are typically separated by about 20° to 30° F. The highs (or lows) vary about 10° to 20° F from the beginning to the end of the month. In transition months like March or September the temperatures may change slightly more than that from the beginning to the end of the month. Even with these possible differences the maps are nonetheless useful to get an overall idea of what range of temperature you should expect in Alaska. More detailed information about temperatures is given in Chapter Two in the climate tables for specific cities. These tables give you average highs and lows, rather than just one averaged temperature per day as the maps do.

The numbers on the precipitation maps from April through December represent inches of water. This includes the water equivalent of any snow which fell in these months. The average water equivalent for fifteen inches of snow in Alaska is about one inch of water, which is very dry snow. The precipitation maps for January through March represent only inches of snow which fell. Any rain which fell in these months is not included in these totals.

Overview of Alaska's Climate

The precipitation maps also show very generalized data. Local precipitation in Alaska is even more variable than temperature. This is because of the large bodies of water, numerous glaciers, and steep, high mountain ranges. The extensive coastline of Alaska is characterized by having moist air which—when it moves inland over the often mountainous terrain—is lifted and cooled, frequently resulting in precipitation. Areas just inland of the first layers of mountains are often rain-shadowed. This scenario is similar to that of the western slope of the Rocky Mountains which gets heavy precipitation and the eastern—rain-shadowed slope—which is a desert (Nevada and Arizona). This situation exists on most of the southern coastline of Alaska and produces significant differences in precipitation over short distances.

Anchorage is a good example of the effect of mountains on precipitation. The precipitation level recorded at the airport (about 14 inches per year) which borders Cook Inlet, is only about half the amount the hillside area (only ten miles away) receives because of the uplift, cooling and increased precipitation as the air rises to get over the Chugach Mountains.

Even though these large-scale precipitation maps cannot show the local differences created by topographic features, they are still useful to show obvious differences between regions of Alaska. I suggest spending a few minutes looking at the following maps to get an overall impression of Alaska's climate and then moving on to Chapter Two for more specific information on areas to which you plan on traveling.

This attractive young woman in summer wear illustrates just how comfortable the weather can be—at times—in Prince William Sound on the Gulf Coast of Alaska.

AVERAGE TEMPERATURES

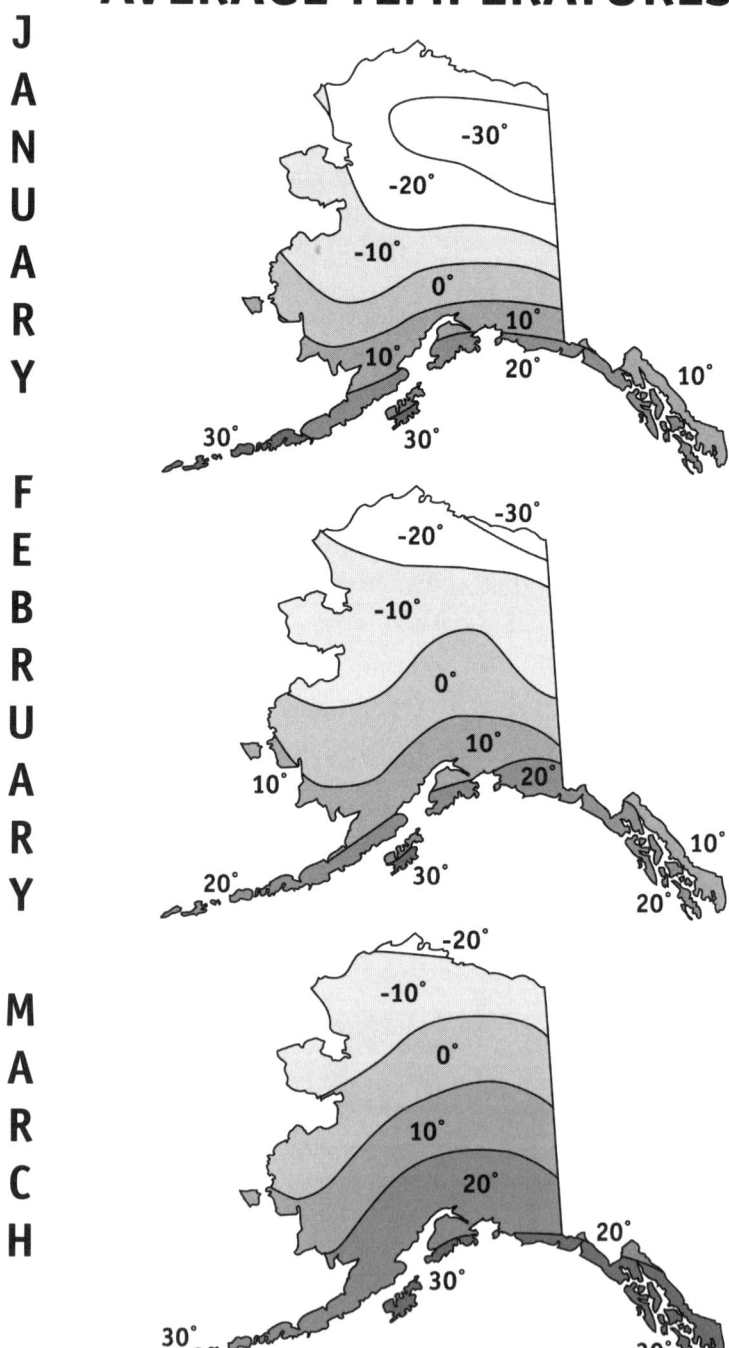

Overview of Alaska's Climate
AVERAGE SNOWFALL

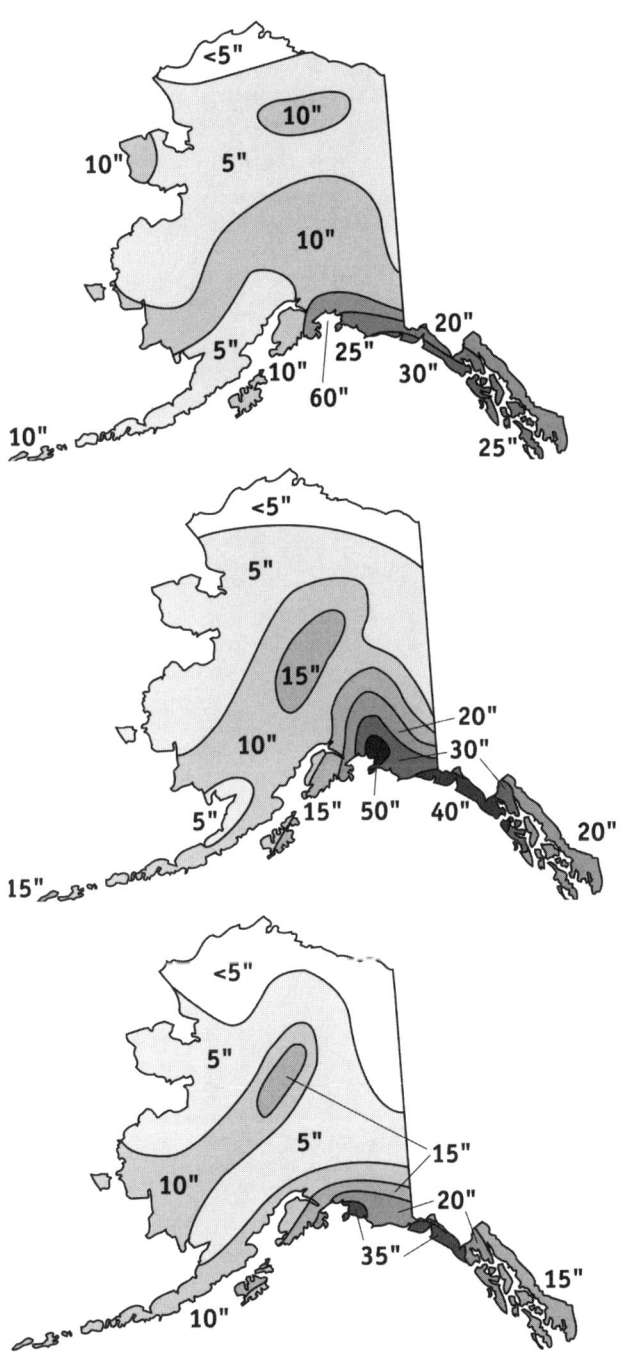

AVERAGE TEMPERATURES

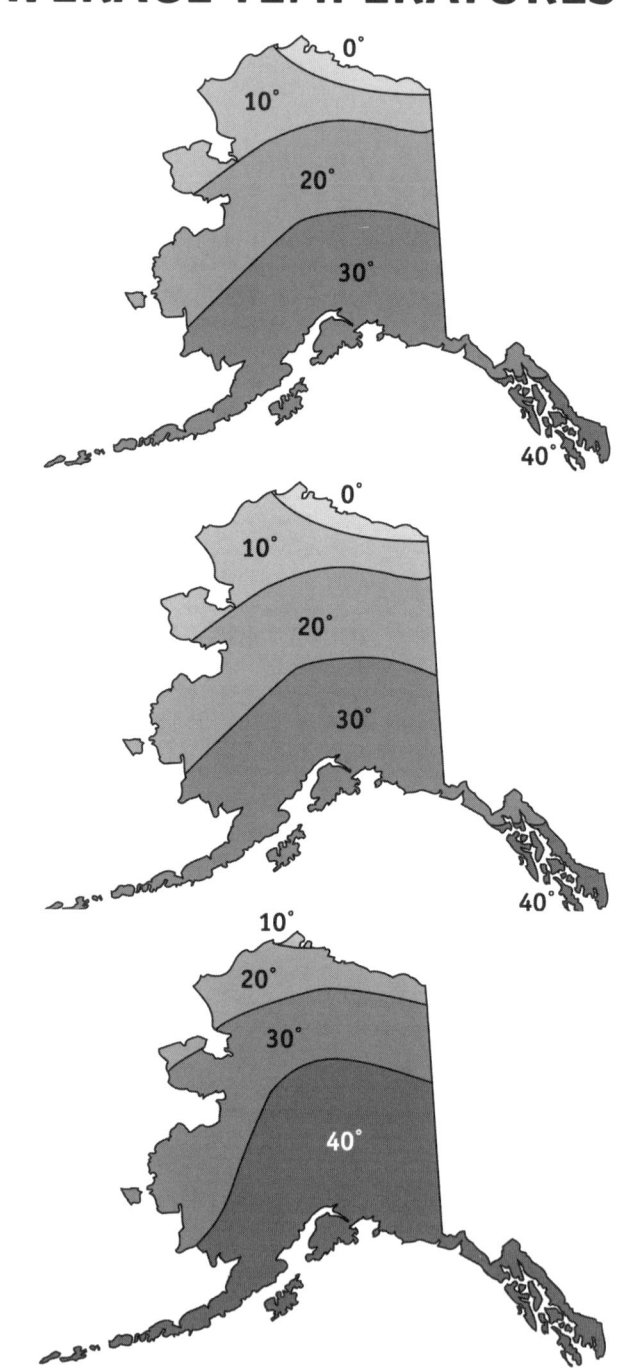

Overview of Alaska's Climate
TOTAL PRECIPITATION

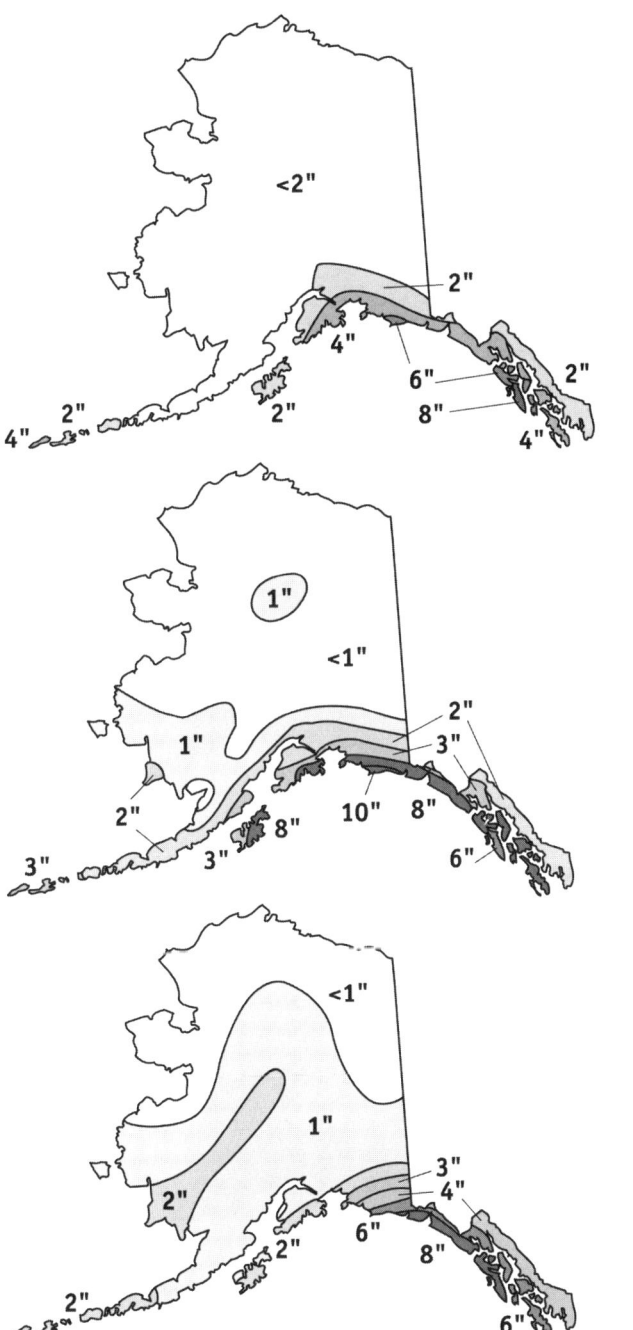

APRIL

MAY

JUNE

AVERAGE TEMPERATURES

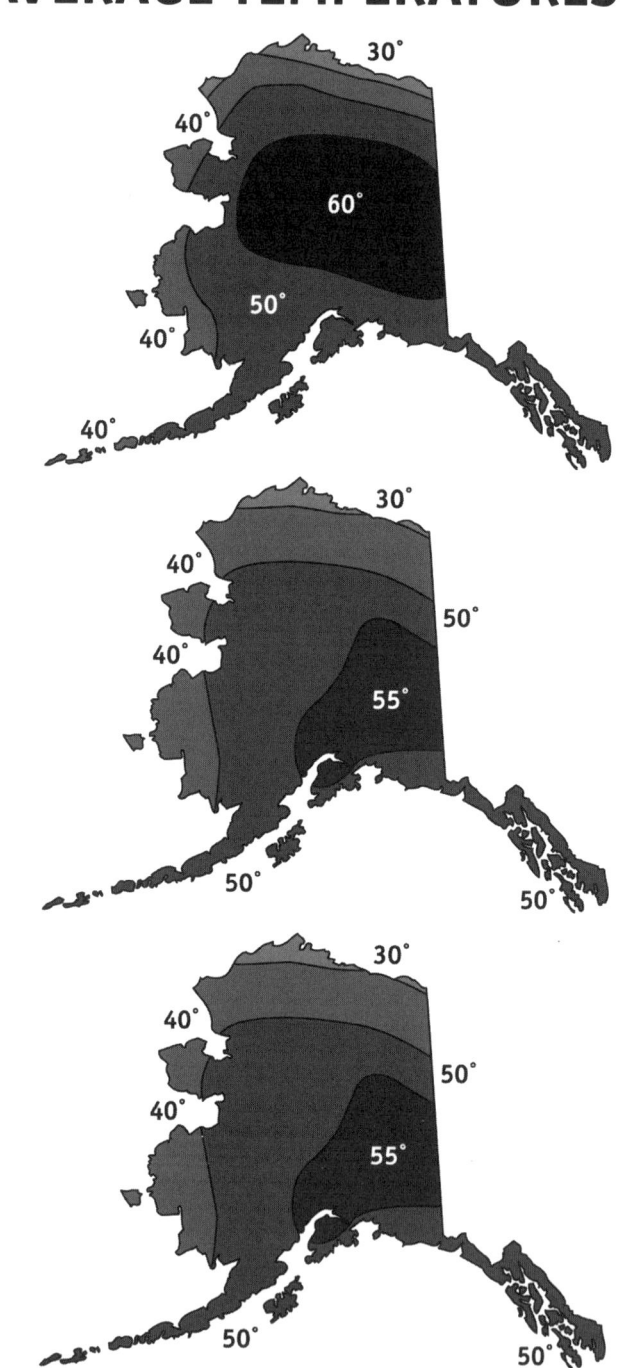

Overview of Alaska's Climate

TOTAL PRECIPITATION

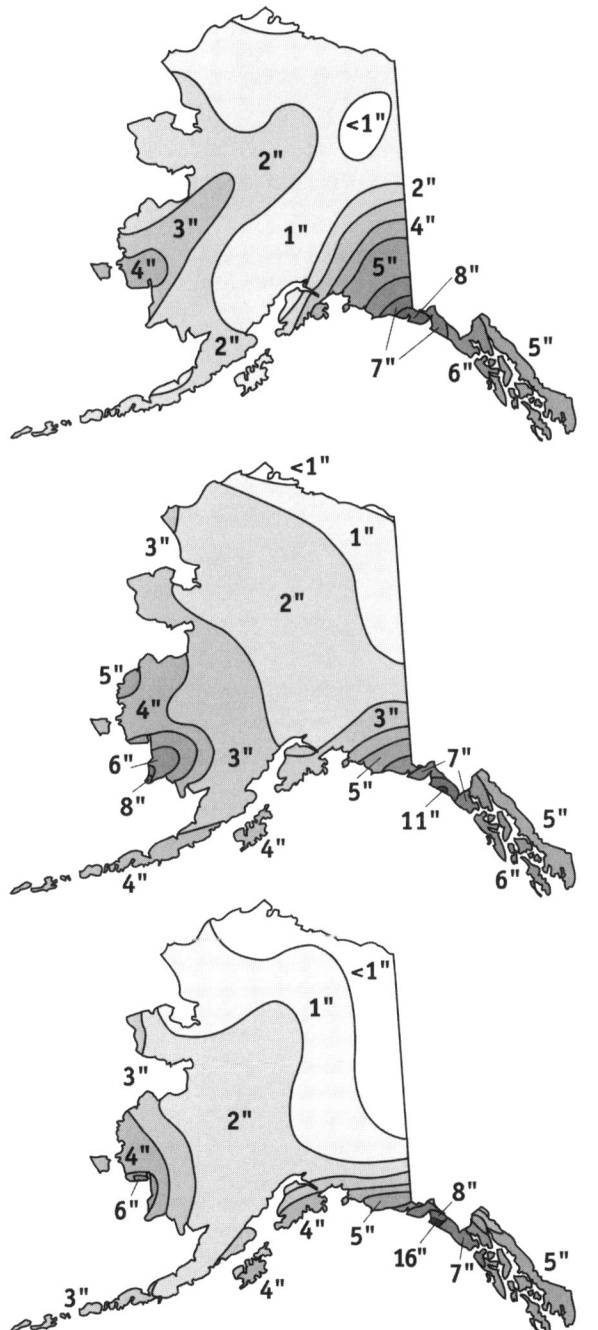

JULY

AUGUST

SEPTEMBER

AVERAGE TEMPERATURES

OCTOBER

NOVEMBER

DECEMBER

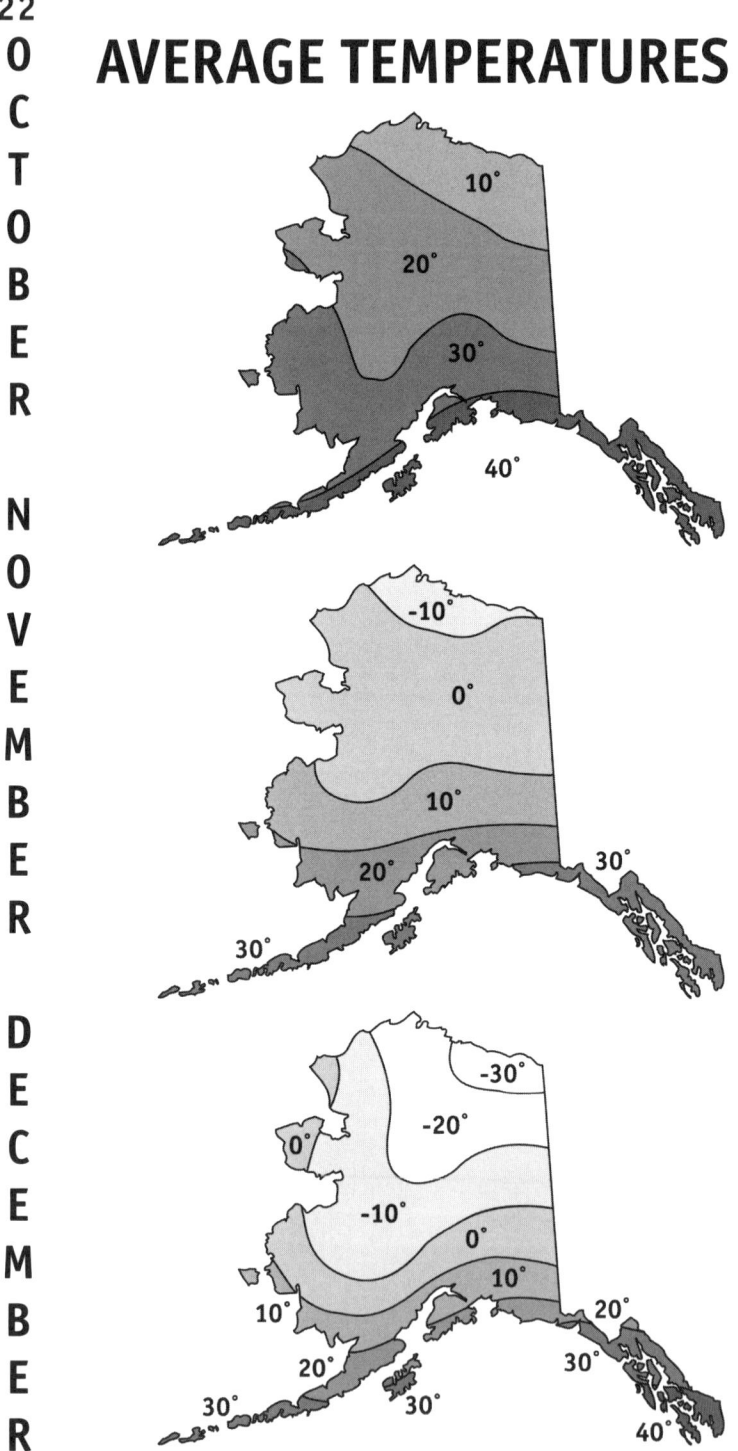

Overview of Alaska's Climate
TOTAL PRECIPITATION

23

OCTOBER

NOVEMBER

DECEMBER

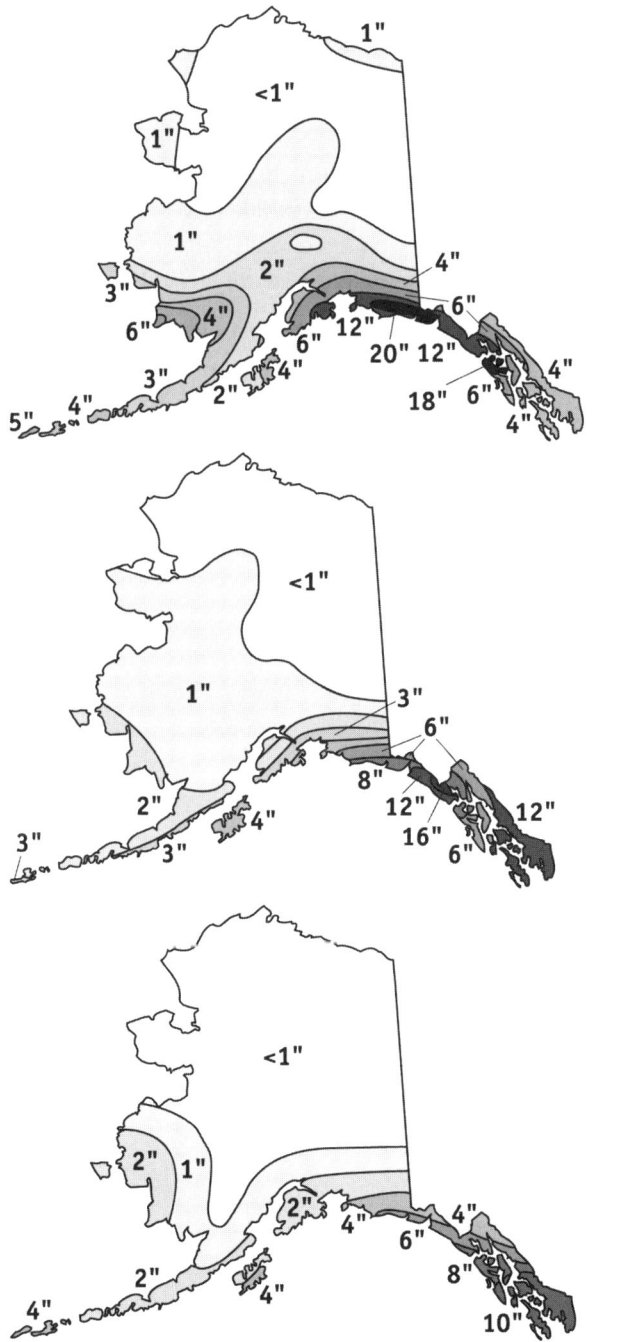

STATEWIDE SUMMARY

Understanding Alaska's weather is difficult because of the size of the state. The Arctic and Interior of Alaska are obviously very cold in winter and cool to warm in summer; in general, the precipitation level in these regions is low. Southcentral, Southwestern and Western Alaska all have more moderate temperatures year round, but they also have more precipitation. Southeastern, the Gulf Coast through Prince William Sound and Kodiak have cool, wet summers and cool, wet winters. Snow tends to melt periodically during winter and precipitation in these areas can be upwards of 200 inches per year.

Having a warm, dry, comfortable experience in Alaska depends on knowing what to pack and then how to dress for the diverse climate. In the next chapter you can find more detailed information about the climate of almost any location in Alaska you wish to visit. Subsequent chapters will deal with choosing the right clothing, footwear and gear for your visit to the 49th state.

CHAPTER TWO

ALASKAN DESTINATIONS

The Alaskan destination(s) you choose as well as the timing of your trip will, at least in part, determine the quality of your experience. The following tables and descriptions of each city's climate has detailed information you can use to plan your trip to fit your needs and expectations. Alaska can be roughly divided into six geographic/climatic regions as shown below.

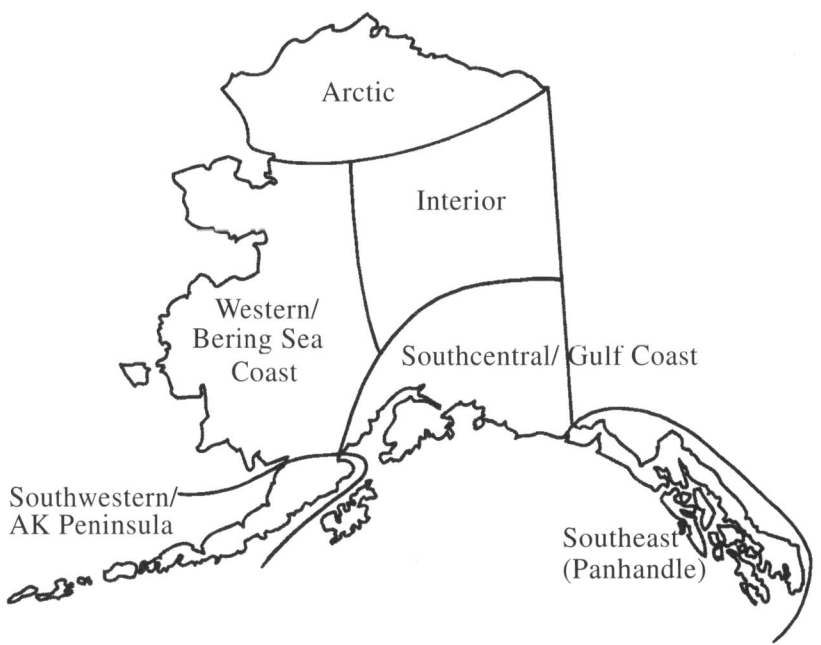

CLIMATE REGIONS
ARCTIC REGION

Arctic destinations include Barrow, Prudhoe Bay and Bettles. All three are above the Arctic Circle. These cities are characterized by cold winters with little snow and little daylight. Summers are cool and short with long days. The Brooks Range runs along the southern border of the Arctic and divides it from the Interior region.

The author resting on a whalebone in the Arctic town of Kotzebue.

INTERIOR REGION

Cities in this region include Fairbanks and McKinley National Park (Denali National Park). Winters are long with plenty of snow and the coldest average temperatures in the state. Summer days can be quite warm with 80° and 90° F days common. This region of Alaska offers some of the best viewing opportunities for the Aurora Borealis.

WESTERN/BERING SEA COAST REGION

Nome, Bethel and McGrath are in this region. It is the largest region in Alaska and has the widest variation in temperature and precipitation. Cities near the coast have more moderate temperatures and higher levels of precipitation. Inland cities in this region tend to be colder and have less precipitation. This region and Southwestern Alaska

Alaskan Destinations

are accessible only by air or water–no roads or railroads connect this area to the rest of the state.

SOUTHWESTERN/ALASKA PENINSULA REGION

King Salmon and Cold Bay are located in this region. It has moderate temperatures, both in winter and summer. The weather factors distinctive of most of this region are regular, high winds and frequent precipitation. Horizontal rain is a common occurrence.

SOUTHCENTRAL/GULF COAST REGION

Anchorage, Gulkana, Homer, Kenai, Kodiak, Talkeetna and Valdez are cities in this region. Winters are generally moderate and summers are relatively long and warm (not hot). Precipitation in summer is not nearly as frequent as in coastal areas and winter snows are substantial with occasional melting periods. This area has the best-developed road system and three-fourths of the state's population.

SOUTHEAST REGION

Juneau (the capital city), Sitka, Wrangell and Ketchikan are located in Southeast. In general, Southeast is the wettest area, especially in winter when rain often falls rather than snow. It also has the most moderate temperatures because of its southern location and proximity to the Northern Pacific Ocean. Southeast Alaska is the most popular destination for visitors, typically via the Inside Passage on one of the many cruise ships servicing Alaska.

CITIES' CLIMATE DESCRIPTIONS & TABLES

The numbers in the following tables represent monthly averages. They represent the level of each climate parameter you would likely find on any day of that month. The averages come from data records from the past 30 to 50 years. Please remember that averages are just that, so weather during a two-week visit may vary from the "average."

The climate descriptions use the following standards:

Spring is March, April and May;
Summer is June, July and August;
Fall is September, October and November;
Winter is December, January and February.

NORMAL MAXIMUM/MINIMUM TEMPERATURE (in Fahrenheit)

These numbers give you a good idea of the high and low temperatures you would experience on an average day in each month. Remember that in Spring and Fall months the daily temperature range will change more from early in the month to late in the month than in Summer and Winter, when the temperatures are more stable. Adding 5 degrees to days early in the month and subtracting 5 degrees from days late in the month is about right for these months of seasonal change. Plus, in the middle of any month, extremes may be 10-15 degrees colder or warmer than these averages. These averages give you a good starting point, but then you will have to allow for some variation up or down from these numbers.

SKY CONDITIONS

Clear, partly cloudy and cloudy indicate sky conditions which existed from sunup to sundown. Clear days were bluebird all day and cloudy days were those without any sun whatsoever. Partly cloudy includes all other sky conditions. If you add the clear days and partly cloudy days the total would give you the number of days per month you would have at least some sunshine, which is a better indicator of nice days in Alaska. Many destinations will have clear skies most of the day except for brief afternoon periods when clouds appear, it rains for a short time, and then the clouds dissipate and the skies are clear again. The proximity to ocean and mountains causes this pattern in many Alaskan locations.

PRECIPITATION DAYS & TOTAL PRECIPITATION

Precipitation days represents the number of days when at least .01 (one-hundredth) of an inch of precipitation fell. Total precipitation is the water equivalent of all forms of precipitation (rain, sleet, snow, etc.) which fell during the month. Even a ten minute sprinkle totaling over .01 inch at 1 a.m. would qualify.

To get a good idea of the wetness of the weather, you should look at total precipitation concurrently with precipitation days. When a city (Anchorage) receives 1.14 inches of rain in June and has 7.9 precipitation days, that means the average rainfall for each precipitation day is only .14 inch, and many of the rainfalls actually amount to less than

Although the frequency of rain is high in many Alaskan destinations, it is often light and doesn't deter people—who dress accordingly—from enjoying the great fishing Alaska has to offer.

one-tenth of one inch. That is not a lot of rain and you will, in fact, only need a raincoat a couple of the most rainy days of June in Anchorage. On the other hand, if you average the clear and cloudy days in with the precipitation days for Ketchikan you will get about .5 inches of rain for every day of the year, which means rainy days usually dump two to three inches of water—or more—and you will often need raingear there or you will get uncomfortably wet.

MONTHLY SNOWFALL

One thing to consider about Alaska's snowfalls is the water equivalent. Alaskan snow is usually dry, and it takes 10 to 20 inches of snow to be the "equivalent" of one inch of water. Of course, wet snowfalls in Spring and Fall contain more water per inch. Also remember the significant influence mountains have on snowfall. Most cities have their weather recording site at the airport on flat ground at some distance from any nearby mountains. Steep hillsides which may also be in town, but ten miles from the airport may have average snowfall depths of two or three times as much as the recording station.

Another easy mistake to make is adding up the winter snowfall to determine the depth of the snow on the ground – snowpack. However, snow settles and packs down considerably after it falls. Also, occasional thaws in many Alaskan locations further reduce the snowpack. Mean temperature, wind levels and humidity are all factors which affect snowpack in a location.

HUMIDITY

These numbers are the 4 p.m. relative humidity given in percentage. A listing of 72 thus means 72% relative humidity–the standard form for humidity measurements. In general, most of Alaska is considered a dry climate although the numbers don't seem that low. Remember it is *relative* humidity, and since Alaska temperatures are cooler than most of the U.S., the *absolute* level of humidity is lower than the numbers might indicate.

AVERAGE WIND SPEED

Because many Alaska destinations are located near large bodies of water and/or mountains, they tend to have windy weather. Wind chill is therefore a major concern when dressing for comfort in Alaska. Wind chill is the term used to describe the cooling effect wind has on us. A 10 mph wind will make the temperature feel about 10 degrees cooler. A 20 mph wind will make it about 20 degrees cooler. (These are both approximations. Wind chill charts are available for more exact comparisons.) Chicago, "The Windy City," has earned a reputation based on how much colder it feels there because of the constant high winds. Many Alaskan cities have the same conditions and reputations.

The wind speeds are recorded in mph for each Alaskan destination. They are averages so they do not take into account how gusty the location can be. For many of these cities, the variability in the wind speed can be found in their written climate descriptions.

DAYLIGHT ON 15TH

Daylight is recorded for the 15th of each month. Day length in Alaska is quite variable between locations and between months of the year because of the north–south dimension of the state. There are several things to keep in mind when looking at the day lengths for each destination:

Alaskan Destinations 31

Alaska–the land of the midnight sun. Even places well south of the Arctic Circle like this one (Wood River, on the western coast), are bathed in light at midnight on the summer solstice because of the low angle at which the sun sets.

- Alaska's sun rises and sets at a low angle to the horizon which produces longer periods of dawn and dusk than experienced in the continental U.S. In Alaska there is more time before dawn and after dusk when it is still light enough for outdoor activity without artificial light.
- Alaska's time zones have been manipulated (in 1983 Alaska went from having four time zones to having only two) to facilitate doing business with the rest of the U.S. Daylight periods are set back one to two hours because of this; i.e. the sun is actually at its zenith between 1 p.m. and 2 p.m. in Alaska; dawn and dusk are similarly affected.
- On the summer solstice (June 20) the more southern destinations like Ketchikan and Cold Bay (about 17 1/2 hours of daylight each) have only a little more light than cities in the northern continental U.S. The only destinations with a true "midnight sun" are those north of the Arctic Circle (Barrow, Bettles and Prudhoe Bay) which is about 66 degrees north Latitude.
- Remember that on March 20 and September 22 every location on Earth has 12 hours of day and 12 hours of night.

AURORA INDEX

The Aurora Borealis, also called the Northern Lights, is a popular attraction for visitors and residents alike. The Aurora Index is a measure of the viewing possibilities at each destination.

The Aurora Borealis is caused by interaction of the Earth's magnetic field and particles from the sun. Aurora activity varies during the night, from night to night, and from season to season. The best time of the evening for viewing is generally 11 p.m. to 1 a.m. The best seasons to see the Aurora are Fall and Spring. Less Aurora activity occurs near the solstices. However, in good locations like Fairbanks or McKinley Park it is commonly seen all Winter. Summer is not a good season because the sunlight interferes with viewing. Artificial light from cities also interferes with viewing so rural areas are better locations for viewing.

The northern Aurora (there is also a southern Aurora visible from Australia) is centered about Fairbanks and residents there often see it straight overhead. The Aurora is visible from the Fairbanks area about 240 nights per year. The Aurora is visible low on the horizon from the northern U.S. in times of extreme activity, but this is not common. Alaskan destinations from Anchorage north to Barrow offer many viewing opportunities each Fall and Spring to see the Aurora. The number of opportunities is determined by: Aurora activity–which is only somewhat predictable less than one week in advance; the condition of the sky–since clouds prevent viewing; and the amount of artificial light present in the viewing area. Near a large city like Anchorage, you must travel some distance (ten to twenty miles from Anchorage) away from the nighttime glow of the city to be able to discern the Aurora.

Southeast Alaska and the Alaska Peninsula do offer some Aurora viewing opportunities during Fall and Spring, but they are too far south to be frequent, good viewing locations.

Photographing the Aurora with good results is difficult. A 35mm camera, normal or wide-angle lens, a tripod, 100 to 400 ASA speed film, a wide-open aperture, 10 to 30-second exposures, and bracketing are recommendations for good results. Other suggestions are focusing on a foreground object about 75 ft. away and remembering to keep the camera as warm as possible whenever not actually taking photos.

Alaskan Destinations 33

During June and July, when the insects can be downright terrible in some locations, it is almost mandatory to wear headnets and gloves to function outdoors. For those who prepare adequately, even in the presence of clouds of insects, this time of year can still be very enjoyable.

BUG INDEX

The Bug Index is a measure of the timing and concentration of biting insects at each destination. There are 25 species of mosquitos in Alaska which feed on people, although none transmit diseases. No-seeums and white sox also abound in many areas of Alaska during the brief summers. The bug season is basically the same as the tourist season—April through September—with June and July being the peak season for both. The most active periods of the day for biting insects are near dawn and dusk. Wind and cool temperatures both decrease their activity. In wet, tundra locations or any areas with substantial amounts of standing water for insect larvae to incubate, the concentrations of biting insects are often high enough to require that people wear head nets and even gloves during any outdoor activity.

~

ANCHORAGE

Anchorage is Alaska's largest city and is located in Southcentral Alaska. Anchorage's weather is moderated significantly by Cook Inlet, which lies to the north, west and south of the city. Maximum summer temperatures seldom exceed 75° F because of the influence of this large body of water. 55° to 65° for June, July and August are expected daytime highs, with occasionally warm days in the 70's.

Another effect of Cook Inlet is that minimum winter temperatures seldom drop below -10° F, especially since the early 1980's when winters have warmed up slightly. Growing up during the 1960's and 70's, it was normal for me to experience at least one period for two to four weeks each winter when the daily low was below -20° F, or even -30°. I can recall only a handful of daily lows below -20° since the late 80's, and during the 90's there have been only a few days each winter below 0° F. Winters have moderated considerably, although summertime temperatures have not gone up. Spring and fall temperatures are cool with early spring/late fall nighttime lows often below freezing.

Precipitation in Anchorage is greatly affected by the Chugach Mountains on the eastern edge of town. This 5,000 ft. to 10,000 ft.

Monthly Summaries	JAN	FEB	MAR	APR	MAY	JUN
normal max. temp. F°	21.4	25.8	33.1	42.8	54.4	61.6
normal min. temp. F°	8.4	11.5	18.1	28.6	38.8	47.2
clear days	7.0	6.7	7.6	5.6	4.0	2.7
partly cloudy days	4.6	3.6	5.4	6.1	6.5	6.9
cloudy days	19.4	18.0	17.9	18.3	20.6	20.4
precipitation days	7.8	7.8	7.4	6.0	7.2	7.9
total precipitation (in.)	0.79	0.7	0.69	0.67	0.73	1.14
monthly snowfall (in.)	10.7	11.5	9.0	4.8	0.4	0.0
4 p.m. relative humidity	72	67	57	53	49	56
average wind speed	6.4	6.9	7.0	7.3	8.4	8.4
daylight on 15th	6:24	7:03	10:43	14:40	17:26	19:17

Alaskan Destinations 35

mountain range prevents moist air from the Gulf of Alaska from reaching Anchorage. As a result, Anchorage receives less than 15 inches of precipitation per year. However, like many Alaskan destinations, summer precipitation comes in the form of numerous continual "drizzles," rather than occasional hard rains. Average snowfall is around 60 to 70 inches, depending on the area of town—the east side near the mountains receiving more than downtown.

Wind in Anchorage is usually light, but gusty periods are common. May and October are better kite months with several gusty days per month. Winter usually brings numerous high wind warnings, particularly on the east side near the foothills and higher elevations. Windstorms with 50 to 80 mph gusts can be expected each winter. Air quality in Anchorage can be poor due to high levels of glacial dust all year and carbon monoxide buildup in winter months.

BUG INDEX: The business districts of town have a small insect population; however, some residential areas can have moderate levels of biting insects in June, July and August.

AURORA INDEX: The glow from the city's lights make viewing the Aurora poor at best. Traveling at least 20 miles north or 10 miles south will make better viewing possible during good displays.

Monthly Summaries	JUL	AUG	SEP	OCT	NOV	DEC
normal max. temp. F°	65.2	63.0	55.2	40.5	27.2	22.5
normal min. temp. F°	51.7	49.5	41.6	28.7	15.1	10.0
clear days	3.4	3.3	3.7	5.0	5.7	5.8
partly cloudy days	5.8	6.1	5.4	4.6	4.7	4.0
cloudy days	21.8	21.6	20.9	21.3	19.6	21.2
precipitation days	11.5	13.4	14.5	12.2	9.6	11.0
total precipitation (in.)	1.71	2.44	2.70	2.03	1.11	1.12
monthly snowfall (in.)	0.0	0.0	0.3	7.3	10.3	14.8
4 p.m. relative humidity	62	64	64	66	73	76
average wind speed	7.3	6.9	6.7	6.7	6.5	6.3
daylight on 15th	18:28	15:52	12:57	10:08	7:19	5:32

BARROW

The most noticeable climate characteristic of Barrow is the temperature–only two months have an average daily low above freezing, and the daily maximum averages over 32° F only about 100 days per year. Snow has been recorded in every month of the year. Barrow's weather is a result of its location on the Arctic Ocean at the northern tip of Alaska. It is often referred to as Point Barrow because of its location at the northern "tip" of Alaska. The ocean is only ice-free for a few months beginning in late July or early August.

The summer high temperatures are "moderated" by the proximity of the Arctic Ocean. This huge body of water also produces an average year-round wind speed of over 11 mph, and there are no nearby physical barriers to block the wind. Gusty winds of 40 to 50 mph can occur in any month. Visitors who venture to Barrow to view the "Midnight Sun" will need at least a light jacket (even in summer) due to the cool temperatures coupled with the constant breeze off the ocean. Winter visitors will need to bring extreme arctic gear to survive the experience.

Monthly Summaries	JAN	FEB	MAR	APR	MAY	JUN
normal max. temp. F°	-7.4	-11.8	-9.0	4.7	24.2	38.3
normal min. temp. F°	-19.3	-23.7	-21.1	-9.1	14.4	29.7
clear days	5.6	11.8	13.7	10.8	3.3	3.5
partly cloudy days	1.5	5.7	6.9	7.0	4.9	5.8
cloudy days	2.6	10.8	10.3	12.3	22.8	20.6
precipitation days	4.4	4.2	3.8	4.1	4.2	4.8
total precipitation (in.)	0.17	0.1	0.17	0.20	0.16	0.28
monthly snowfall (in.)	2.2	2.1	1.8	2.1	0.6	0.5
4 p.m. relative humidity	69	66	68	76	86	89
average wind speed	11.7	11.2	11.2	11.5	11.9	11.5
daylight on 15th	00:00	1:55	11:30	16:30	24:00	24:00

Alaskan Destinations 37

Like many parts of Alaska, Barrow has only a few entirely clear days each summer, although winter months tend to be much clearer. The long daylight in summer tends to bring clouds, precipitation and fog with it. Visitors should bring rainwear for late summer and early fall trips.

On November 18th, the sun sets in Barrow and doesn't rise again until January 24th–66 days without the sun being up. However, because the sun travels at a low angle to the horizon, there are still many hours of twilight for weeks after the sun sets and before it rises again. Barrow is in total darkness for about half of the time the sun is down. After the sun rises on May 10th, it doesn't set again until August 2nd.

BUG INDEX: High in July and August, although the wind helps keep them from being as intense as areas farther inland.

AURORA INDEX: Barrow is a good place to view the Aurora in late winter because of its northern position, the lack of artificial light and the clear skies at that time of year.

note: The clear/cloudy/partly cloudy days in the table don't add up to 30 or 31 during months of darkness due to the inability to determine sky conditions.

Monthly Summaries	JUL	AUG	SEP	OCT	NOV	DEC
normal max. temp. F°	45.0	42.3	33.8	18.1	3.5	-5.2
normal min. temp. F°	33.6	33.3	27.0	8.8	-6.9	-17.2
clear days	3.5	1.4	1.2	2.3	5.6	3.6
partly cloudy days	7.0	3.9	2.6	3.9	2.6	0.0
cloudy days	20.5	25.7	26.2	24.9	10.7	0.0
precipitation days	8.7	10.7	10.5	11.0	6.1	4.9
total precipitation (in.)	0.94	0.96	0.60	0.45	0.25	0.16
monthly snowfall (in.)	0.5	0.7	3.6	6.7	3.4	2.5
4 p.m. relative humidity	84	86	87	84	78	71
average wind speed	11.7	12.4	13.2	13.3	12.4	11.6
daylight on 15th	24:00	18:54	13:32	8:52	2:40	00:00

BETHEL

Located on the Kuskokwim River in Western Alaska, Bethel's weather patterns are affected both by the Bering Sea to the southwest and mainland Alaska to the east. Most of the year Bethel is influenced by weather funneled through mountains coming from the Bering Sea, producing a maritime climate. Cool early summer temperatures in the 50's are normal and early winter temperatures are still moderate–averaging above 20° F even into late November. Wind speeds average above 10 mph all year due to the lack of any protective barriers nearby. Winter winds average above 14 mph, making the city seem colder than the ambient air temperatures would indicate.

In June and July, warm air coming from the east raises daytime temperatures to an average above 60° F and it is not uncommon for temperatures to reach 70° F during July. These warm temperatures result in a few severe thunderstorms this time of year. Due to the maritime influence, skies are cloudy much of the summer, with only a few clear days per month. In December and January, inland air also affects Bethel, but this time it is a colder air mass which reduces the average temperature–resulting in an average low of around 0° F.

Monthly Summaries	JAN	FEB	MAR	APR	MAY	JUN
normal max. temp. F°	12.9	12.8	21.1	31.3	48.2	58.8
normal min. temp. F°	0.4	-0.8	5.4	15.7	31.7	42.3
clear days	8.0	9.9	9.3	6.4	3.6	1.7
partly cloudy days	4.7	4.1	5.3	6.3	7.7	6.9
cloudy days	18.3	14.2	16.5	17.3	19.6	21.4
precipitation days	8.6	6.7	9.2	8.8	10.5	12.6
total precipitation (in.)	0.58	0.43	0.59	0.70	0.78	1.44
monthly snowfall (in.)	5.8	5.5	7.6	5.3	1.9	0.1
4 p.m. relative humidity	76	73	74	72	62	61
average wind speed	14.6	15.2	14.0	12.9	11.6	11.2
daylight on 15th	6:30	9:06	11:43	14:38	17:20	19:07

Alaskan Destinations 39

Moist air moving north from the Bering sea produces more precipitation in late summer. Bethel gets half of its annual 15-inch average in July, August and September. Bethel gets an average snowfall of around 50 inches, beginning in October and continuing until April. However, storms directed northeast from the Bering Sea often bring strong winter winds exceeding 50 mph which reduce snow depths. Bethel also gets frequent, warm, southerly winter winds (Chinooks) which raise temperatures above the freezing mark and further reduce snow accumulations.

CITIES WITH SIMILAR CLIMATE: Mountain Village, Aniak.

BUG INDEX: Although the breeze along the river helps keep the insects at bay, June, July and August can have very high populations of biting insects.

AURORA INDEX: Good Aurora displays are possible over Bethel from early fall until late spring.

Monthly Summaries	JUL	AUG	SEP	OCT	NOV	DEC
normal max. temp. F°	62.3	59.5	52.0	35.0	22.6	14.7
normal min. temp. F°	47.7	46.3	38.3	23.8	10.9	2.2
clear days	1.8	1.5	2.3	3.6	5.7	7.8
partly cloudy days	5.4	4.0	4.9	5.3	5.0	4.9
cloudy days	23.7	25.5	22.7	22.1	19.3	18.3
precipitation days	15.1	17.7	16.1	12.6	11.5	10.9
total precipitation (in.)	1.98	2.91	2.04	1.45	1.07	1.02
monthly snowfall (in.)	T	0.0	0.3	4.1	8.7	9.7
4 p.m. relative humidity	67	73	70	76	80	77
average wind speed	10.9	11.1	11.7	12.6	13.5	14.2
daylight on 15th	18:19	15:48	12:57	10:09	7:24	5:41

40
BETTLES

Bettles is located on the southern slope of the Brooks Range, just north of the Arctic Circle. It has a typical continental climate–cold winters and (relatively) warm summers. Temperatures often reach -40° or -50° F in winter and occasionally surpass 80° in summer. Winds are light and seldom strong.

Precipitation levels are higher than many interior Alaskan locations, but still lower than most of the continental U.S. Precipitation increases during late summer and early fall months, which is a common pattern in Alaska.

Since Bettles is north of the Arctic Circle it does have a time from June 2nd to July 9th when the sun is constantly up. There is also a corresponding period of time around the winter solstice (Dec. 21) when there is continual darkness for about 38 days.

BUG INDEX: Very high insect levels from June through August.

AURORA INDEX: Very good viewing from fall to spring.

Monthly Summaries	JAN	FEB	MAR	APR	MAY	JUN
normal max. temp. F°	-4.9	0.3	14.4	31.5	52.9	67.5
normal min. temp. F°	-20.4	-18.3	-8.6	9.7	33.5	47.0
clear days	14.8	9.8	9.4	7.2	6.8	3.8
partly cloudy days	5.2	4.2	5.4	9.8	11.0	13.4
cloudy days	11.0	14.0	16.2	13.0	13.2	12.8
precipitation days	7.5	6.7	7.7	5.3	6.6	10.0
total precipitation (in.)	0.69	0.64	0.68	0.64	0.61	1.44
monthly snowfall (in.)	12.5	9.4	10.5	7.2	1.2	T
4 p.m. relative humidity	67	63	61	60	51	48
average wind speed	6.1	6.4	7.1	7.5	7.5	7.5
daylight on 15th	4:00	8:06	11:36	15:29	19:38	24:00

Alaskan Destinations 41

Like many destinations in Alaska, Bettles has a lot of tundra and rain. Dressing appropriately with high-quality rainwear will allow you to keep a smile on your face, too.

Monthly Summaries	JUL	AUG	SEP	OCT	NOV	DEC
normal max. temp. F°	69.6	62.7	49.0	24.9	5.1	-1.8
normal min. temp. F°	49.2	43.8	32.4	12.1	-8.8	-16.7
clear days	2.0	2.2	6.6	4.6	9.4	9.0
partly cloudy days	9.8	8.2	7.0	5.8	6.2	6.6
cloudy days	19.2	20.6	16.4	20.6	14.4	15.4
precipitation days	11.0	13.5	11.3	11.4	9.9	10.1
total precipitation (in.)	1.94	2.38	1.72	1.20	0.90	0.90
monthly snowfall (in.)	0.0	0.1	1.8	11.9	13.2	15.1
4 p.m. relative humidity	54	62	63	73	73	71
average wind speed	6.7	6.3	6.7	6.6	6.0	5.8
daylight on 15th	21:58	17:09	13:14	9:34	5:34	1:54

COLD BAY

Cold Bay is located at the southwest end of the Alaska Peninsula–bordered by the Pacific Ocean to the southeast and the Bering Sea to the northwest. With all this water around it is no surprise that the climate is basically maritime. Summers are cool and winters are very moderate. The seasons are also about a month later than many Alaskan cities because of the effect of nearby water bodies. The warmest month is August and the coldest is February.

Cold Bay is famous for its steady wind as well as frequent windstorms at any time of the year. With an average wind speed of about 17 mph—slightly less than that of the "Windy City" (Chicago), Cold Bay's winds are cold and biting. The town also experiences gusty winds over 60 mph most months of the year. Cloud cover is 100% from sunup to sundown on at least 220 days per year, and there are only about a dozen clear days each year.

Measurable precipitation falls over 280 days per year. However, the average amount per day is only 1/6 of an inch. As at many Alaska destinations, outdoor activity often continues rain or shine, because the rain is often just a light drizzle.

Monthly Summaries	JAN	FEB	MAR	APR	MAY	JUN
normal max. temp. F°	33.1	32.0	34.8	37.9	44.4	50.4
normal min. temp. F°	24.1	22.8	25.0	28.6	34.8	40.9
clear days	2.4	1.9	1.9	0.6	0.5	0.4
partly cloudy days	5.5	4.6	5.9	3.8	2.8	2.6
cloudy days	23.1	21.8	23.2	25.6	27.7	27.0
precipitation days	19.0	17.3	18.0	16.1	17.4	16.0
total precipitation (in.)	2.84	2.27	2.1	1.97	2.29	2.10
monthly snowfall (in.)	10.5	11.4	10.3	5.9	1.7	0.0
4 p.m. relative humidity	83	81	78	77	76	78
average wind speed	17.6	17.8	17.3	17.6	16.1	15.8
daylight on 15th	7:47	9:45	11:50	14:10	16:13	17:23

Alaskan Destinations 43

CITIES WITH SIMILAR CLIMATES: Sand Point, King Cove.

BUG INDEX: Moderate at worst–constant winds lower their ferocity.

AURORA INDEX: Fair viewing possibilities on the rare clear nights from late fall to early spring.

Cold Bay is one of many coastal destinations in Alaska where–if the sun shines and the wind lets up—you should take advantage of it, because you never know when—and if—it will happen again.

Monthly Summaries	JUL	AUG	SEP	OCT	NOV	DEC
normal max. temp. F°	55.1	55.9	52.2	44.3	38.9	35.3
normal min. temp. F°	46.0	47.1	43.2	34.8	29.9	26.6
clear days	0.2	0.2	0.3	0.7	1.1	1.6
partly cloudy days	2.3	1.9	3.5	5.2	5.4	5.3
cloudy days	28.5	28.9	26.3	25.2	23.5	24.1
precipitation days	16.9	19.9	20.7	22.7	21.6	20.6
total precipitation (in.)	2.52	3.24	4.41	4.34	4.19	3.67
monthly snowfall (in.)	T	0.0	0.0	2.9	7.7	10.3
4 p.m. relative humidity	82	83	80	77	80	83
average wind speed	15.7	16.4	16.3	16.8	17.5	17.5
daylight on 15th	16:50	14:59	12:43	10:28	8:21	7:10

44
FAIRBANKS

Fairbanks is located in Interior Alaska and is the second largest city in the state. It has a typical continental climate with large temperature swings from summer to winter. Summer high temperatures average above 70° F in June and July and daily temperatures surpass the 80° mark ten or more times in an average summer. Winter temperature minimums average below zero from November through March.

The greatest temperature swing occurs in winter when the range is from -65° F to 45° above zero. The extreme temperature range occurs because of frigid Arctic air which moves in from the north and warm air which moves in from the south off the Gulf of Alaska. Chinook winds from the Alaska Range to the south often accompany this warm air from the Gulf–intensifying the rise in temperature.

Fairbanks receives snowfall in small amounts from October through April, but most of it persists all winter. Like many locations in Alaska, the snow is very dry so the 70 inches is the equivalent of only four or five inches of water. During each of the summer months, Fairbanks gets an inch or two of rain, with July and August being the wettest months.

Monthly Summaries	JAN	FEB	MAR	APR	MAY	JUN
normal max. temp. F°	-1.6	7.2	23.8	41.0	59.3	70.1
normal min. temp. F°	-18.5	-14.4	-1.7	20.4	38.0	49.5
clear days	9.0	8.3	9.8	6.5	4.5	2.9
partly cloudy days	5.9	5.9	6.8	7.8	11.0	10.3
cloudy days	16.2	14.1	14.4	15.7	15.5	16.8
precipitation days	7.6	6.7	6.0	4.6	6.9	10.8
total precipitation (in.)	0.47	0.40	0.37	0.32	0.61	1.37
monthly snowfall (in.)	10.8	8.6	6.6	3.4	0.8	T
4 p.m. relative humidity	69	63	53	46	38	43
average wind speed	3.1	4.0	5.3	6.6	7.7	7.1
daylight on 15th	5:06	8:30	11:39	15:09	16:38	21:39

Alaskan Destinations 45

Fairbanks' weather is affected by the hills surrounding it. Summer thunderstorms occur about ten days each summer, but are much more frequent in the hills to the east and north of Fairbanks. Fairbanks also experiences frequent periods of ice fog in winter as colder air gets trapped in the valley holding the city. Precipitation is also lighter in town than the surrounding hills, because the hills cause moving air masses to rise, cool and release their moisture.

Winds are light in Fairbanks and windstorms are very infrequent. In winter, Fairbanks becomes an urban heat island, with temperatures as much as 15° warmer than surrounding areas.

CITIES WITH SIMILAR CLIMATES: North Pole, Delta Junction, Chena Hot Springs, Manley Hot Springs.

BUG INDEX: Biting insects are moderately heavy in the downtown district, but can be dense in outlying areas from late May through early September.

AURORA INDEX: Excellent viewing during good displays from late fall through late spring as long as you travel away from the city's glow. The Aurora is visible from Fairbanks an average of 240 nights per year. The city sits directly under the Aurora's center.

Monthly Summaries	JUL	AUG	SEP	OCT	NOV	DEC
normal max. temp. F°	72.3	66.3	54.8	32.0	10.9	1.8
normal min. temp. F°	52.6	47.2	36.2	18.1	-5.6	-14.8
clear days	3.4	3.0	4.2	3.9	7.0	6.8
partly cloudy days	9.2	6.9	6.1	5.0	5.1	5.8
cloudy days	18.6	21.2	19.7	22.1	17.9	18.4
precipitation days	12.2	12.3	9.6	10.7	10.4	9.9
total precipitation (in.)	1.87	1.96	0.95	0.90	0.80	0.85
monthly snowfall (in.)	T	T	1.6	10.9	13.6	13.8
4 p.m. relative humidity	50	54	55	67	73	72
average wind speed	6.6	6.2	6.2	5.4	3.9	3.2
daylight on 15th	20:02	16:36	13:07	9:48	6:21	4:49

GULKANA

Located in the interior, Gulkana has a typical continental climate, but with slightly less extreme temperatures than Fairbanks. The winters aren't quite as cold, with average minimums for all months above zero. Average summer high temperatures in the warmest months—July and August—are in the mid to upper 60's. Daily extremes do occasionally reach 80° F in summer and less than -40° F in winter.

Precipitation is relatively low for the year because the Chugach Mountains to the south act as a barrier. Most of the moisture coming off the Gulf of Alaska is dropped on the southern side of these mountains before reaching Gulkana. The total precipitation for the year is less than 12 inches, but the frequency of occurrence is high. Gulkana receives over .01 inches about 100 days per year. Winds are generally light around Gulkana and strong winds are rare.

CITIES WITH SIMILAR CLIMATE: Glennallen, Copper Center, Chitina, Paxson.

BUG INDEX: Be prepared for high levels of biting insects all summer in areas near Gulkana.

Monthly Summaries	JAN	FEB	MAR	APR	MAY	JUN
normal max. temp. F°	2.5	13.6	28.1	41.5	54.8	64.2
normal min. temp. F°	-13.9	-7.0	2.6	19.9	32.6	42.2
clear days	14.8	6.2	9.4	5.0	3.0	2.0
partly cloudy days	4.4	4.4	6.4	9.8	9.8	10.0
cloudy days	11.8	17.8	15.2	15.2	18.2	18.0
precipitation days	7.3	5.7	5.0	2.8	5.1	9.6
total precipitation (in.)	0.45	0.53	0.36	0.24	0.61	1.60
monthly snowfall (in.)	10.8	8.6	6.6	3.4	0.8	T
4 p.m. relative humidity	71	66	54	46	40	43
average wind speed	5.1	5.6	6.5	8.6	8.8	8.8
daylight on 15th	6:07	8:58	11:46	14:53	17:48	19:50

Alaskan Destinations 47

AURORA INDEX: Good viewing opportunities for the Aurora from late fall to early spring all around Gulkana.

Hip boots for wading, long-sleeve shirt to discourage insects, sunglasses and a billed cap to keep the sun out of your eyes–and you are set to pursue king salmon on the Gulkana River.

Monthly Summaries	JUL	AUG	SEP	OCT	NOV	DEC
normal max. temp. F°	68.3	64.7	54.1	35.3	12.7	4.6
normal min. temp. F°	46.4	42.2	33.4	19.3	-2.5	-10.9
clear days	4.4	2.6	5.6	3.0	4.6	6.8
partly cloudy days	9.0	9.4	7.8	6.8	4.6	6.8
cloudy days	17.6	19.0	16.6	21.2	20.8	17.4
precipitation days	12.7	11.5	10.8	8.5	7.5	8.1
total precipitation (in.)	1.78	1.50	1.38	0.89	0.61	0.92
monthly snowfall (in.)	T	T	1.6	10.9	13.6	13.8
4 p.m. relative humidity	49	50	53	67	76	75
average wind speed	8.2	8.0	7.6	6.3	4.8	3.6
daylight on 15th	18:49	16:00	12:56	9:58	7:00	5:06

48
HOMER

Homer is situated in southcentral Alaska near the tip of the Kenai Peninsula. The town sits on the edge of Kachemak Bay near its confluence with Cook Inlet. Homer has a typical (Alaskan) marine climate.

Summers in Homer are mild with the warmest months averaging only 60° F. Daily high temperatures seldom surpass 70°. Summertime temperatures can be cool for any outdoor activity because of the proximity to the ocean. Also because of the ocean, winter minimum temperatures seldom drop below zero, with the lowest month's average in the mid-teens and daytime highs near the freezing mark. Because of this, snow levels often shrink during winter and leave little accumulation right in town. The nearby hills do, however, maintain snow for the entire winter.

Precipitation in Homer is less than most coastal Alaskan cities to the south because of the Kenai Mountains which act as a barrier to moisture coming from the Gulf of Alaska. The months with the most frequent occurrence of precipitation—September and October—have

Monthly Summaries	JAN	FEB	MAR	APR	MAY	JUN
normal max. temp. F°	28.5	31.2	35.9	42.2	50.0	56.3
normal min. temp. F°	16.8	18.1	21.9	28.6	35.6	42.2
clear days	7.7	6.8	6.1	5.4	3.7	3.9
partly cloudy days	4.2	4.4	6.3	6.3	6.8	8.1
cloudy days	19.1	17.1	18.7	18.3	20.5	17.9
precipitation days	13.4	11.3	11.2	9.4	9.7	9.0
total precipitation (in.)	2.40	2.13	1.70	1.28	1.15	1.03
monthly snowfall (in.)	10.3	12.1	9.4	3.2	0.4	T
4 p.m. relative humidity	76	71	66	65	65	67
average wind speed	8.3	8.1	8.1	8.1	8.3	8.0
daylight on 15th	6:48	9:12	11:48	14:34	17:06	18:42

Alaskan Destinations 49

only about 15 days of measurable rain (which is low by Alaskan standards).

With about 25 inches of precipitation per year, Homer gets only about two-thirds of what Seattle does (34 inches per year). Humidity in Homer is also lower than would be expected for a maritime climate with 65% to 70% all year.

Homer gets an above average amount of sun by Alaskan standards. With less than 20 days of sunup to sundown overcast skies, it has what is considered a sunny climate–for Alaska. Homer is a favorite summer destination for residents and visitors alike because of its favorable weather.

Homer generally has a light ocean breeze but seldom gets strong winds. However, ocean travelers who depart the Homer docks and travel just a few miles out can experience strong winds at any time of year.

CITIES WITH SIMILAR CLIMATE: Seldovia, Anchor Point.

BUG INDEX: Low to moderate.

AURORA INDEX: Good viewing possibilities from late fall to early spring.

Monthly Summaries	JUL	AUG	SEP	OCT	NOV	DEC
normal max. temp. F°	60.5	60.4	54.7	43.8	34.5	30.1
normal min. temp. F°	46.2	46.2	40.5	31.2	22.6	18.4
clear days	3.3	5.3	4.8	5.2	5.9	7.4
partly cloudy days	8.6	7.7	7.0	5.2	5.3	5.3
cloudy days	19.1	18.1	18.1	20.6	18.9	18.3
precipitation days	11.2	12.7	15.5	15.2	12.2	15.0
total precipitation (in.)	1.49	2.24	3.29	3.24	2.62	2.82
monthly snowfall (in.)	0.0	0.0	0.0	2.1	7.3	13.0
4 p.m. relative humidity	71	72	70	69	74	77
average wind speed	7.4	6.7	7.2	7.6	8.1	8.0
daylight on 15th	17:55	15:33	12:51	10:11	7:35	6:03

JUNEAU

Juneau is a typical southeastern Alaska city in both topography and climate. Juneau sits precariously on the edge of the Coast Mountains as they meet the myriad inland bays within the inside passage– basically part of the Northern Pacific Ocean. It has a marine climate with mild winters, cool summers, little sunshine and abundant precipitation.

Just to the east of Juneau lies the Coast Mountains consisting of rugged peaks and numerous glaciers. This mountain range and the Gulf of Alaska to the northwest largely determine Juneau's weather. Storms from the Gulf bring in plenty of precipitation and the mountains regularly send strong winds whistling through the glacial valleys and passages leading to Juneau.

Summer maximum temperatures average only into the low 60's with an occasional high reading of 80° F. Evenings are cool because of the maritime influence.

Winter temperatures average barely below freezing during December and January and already begin to warm up in late February.

Monthly Summaries	JAN	FEB	MAR	APR	MAY	JUN
normal max. temp. F°	29.4	34.1	38.7	47.2	55.1	60.9
normal min. temp. F°	19.0	22.7	26.7	32.1	38.9	45.0
clear days	5.4	4.4	4.3	3.6	3.7	3.4
partly cloudy days	2.7	2.8	3.1	4.2	4.2	4.0
cloudy days	22.8	21.0	23.6	22.2	23.1	22.5
precipitation days	18.5	16.6	18.0	16.8	17.1	15.5
total precipitation (in.)	4.54	3.75	3.28	2.77	3.42	3.15
monthly snowfall (in.)	26.0	19.0	14.9	3.5	0.0	T
4 p.m. relative humidity	78	75	68	63	63	65
average wind speed	8.1	8.4	8.4	8.6	8.3	7.7
daylight on 15th	7:06	9:22	11:44	14:23	16:45	18:15

Alaskan Destinations 51

Juneau averages only one day per year when the minimum temperature is below zero. It does experience short periods of comparatively severe weather in winter when glacial winds funneling from Canada over Juneau's ice fields cause the wind chill to be well below the zero mark. The associated winds are known as Taku winds and can cause significant damage in both Juneau and nearby Douglas Island.

Precipitation in Juneau is heavy and regular. June has the fewest days without precipitation, but still has over 15 days with a measurable amount. October averages over 23 days with precipitation. The average yearly total is 54 inches. There are, however, clear periods of two or more days during almost every month that give some relief from the overcast skies. Even October which averages over 7 inches of rain, has at least a couple bluebird days to break up the gloomy skies. As in the rest of Southeast, residents of Juneau go on with their outdoor activities in spite of wet weather.

CITIES WITH SIMILAR CLIMATE: Hoonah, Haines, Yakutat.

BUG INDEX: Moderate levels in summer months–low otherwise.

AURORA INDEX: Juneau's southerly location makes it only a fair location from which to view the Aurora. Fall and spring are best.

Monthly Summaries	JUL	AUG	SEP	OCT	NOV	DEC
normal max. temp. F°	63.9	62.7	55.9	47.1	36.7	31.6
normal min. temp. F°	48.1	47.3	42.9	37.2	27.2	22.6
clear days	2.9	4.0	2.7	2.4	3.3	3.4
partly cloudy days	4.6	4.7	3.3	2.0	2.2	2.0
cloudy days	23.4	22.3	24.0	26.6	24.5	25.6
precipitation days	16.7	17.4	20.4	23.5	20.1	21.1
total precipitation (in.)	4.16	5.32	6.73	7.84	4.91	4.44
monthly snowfall (in.)	0.0	0.0	T	1.1	11.9	22.6
4 p.m. relative humidity	70	74	78	79	81	83
average wind speed	7.5	7.4	8.0	9.5	8.5	8.9
daylight on 15th	17:37	15:26	12:52	10:21	7:53	6:25

KENAI

Kenai is located at the base of the Kenai Peninsula in Southcentral Alaska. Its climate is influenced by nearby Cook Inlet more than anything else. Consequently, it has relatively mild winters and cool summers. Summertime maximum temperatures rarely exceed 80° F, with the average for the warmest months only 61° F (July and August).

Winter temperatures are mild for Alaska with no month averaging below zero. Kenai is not located in close proximity to a mountain range so it seldom gets the strong winter winds as do many Alaskan cities surrounded by mountains.

Precipitation is heaviest from July through September, with May being the driest month–and the sunniest. Total annual precipitation is less than 20 inches and Kenai tends to get its rain in larger doses than most southcentral locations. This equates to fewer drizzly days–the rain tends to do its thing and then the sun can come out.

Winter snowfall and accumulation varies quite a bit around Kenai because of the winter warming spells, particularly since about 1980. Some years will have only 30 inches of accumulation and others will have over 60 inches.

CITIES WITH SIMILAR CLIMATE: Soldotna, Clam Gulch, Ninilchik, Sterling.

BUG INDEX: High in June and July. Can be high in August if the weather stays warm.

AURORA INDEX: Viewing can be good in areas away from the city's glow beginning in late fall and continuing to early spring.

Monthly Summaries	JAN	FEB	MAR	APR	MAY	JUN
normal max. temp. F°	21	26	32	42	52	58
normal min. temp. F°	3	6	11	23	35	42
total precipitation (in.)	0.9	0.9	0.9	0.8	0.8	1.1
monthly snowfall (in.)	12.5	10.9	9.8	5	0.0	0.0
daylight on 15th	6:38	9:11	11:47	14:40	17:20	19:02

Alaskan Destinations 53

Whether it's a sunny summer day (left) or a cold fall afternoon (below), fishermen dressed for the weather will always enjoy the world-famous fishing on the Kenai River.

Monthly Summaries	JUL	AUG	SEP	OCT	NOV	DEC
normal max. temp. F°	61	61	55	43	30	21
normal min. temp. F°	46	45	38	28	15	5
total precipitation (in.)	2.3	3.1	3.4	2.1	1.6	1.1
monthly snowfall (in.)	0.0	0.0	0.0	2.8	8.9	13.6
daylight on 15th	18:12	15:41	12:52	10:07	7:23	5:45

KETCHIKAN

Ketchikan's claim to fame is its high level of precipitation. This Southeast city which sits at the southern tip of Alaska's Panhandle gets over 150 inches of precipitation per year–95% of that in the form of rain. The town is in a northern rain forest (Tongass National Forest) and has a (wet) marine climate.

Summer temperatures are moderate with average highs in the mid-60's. Although evenings don't cool off much, the damp climate requires adequate clothing to be comfortable. Head-to-toe raingear and waterproof footwear is standard attire for residents; visitors would be wise to follow their lead.

Winters are very mild because of the maritime influence. Temperatures are only subfreezing for three winter months—December through February—and then only at night. Daytime averages for these months are still above the freezing mark. Although Ketchikan does get over 30 inches of snow each winter, most of that is wet snow which doesn't persist all winter. Most snowfalls melt away within a week.

Winds can be strong and gusty and often accompany the plentiful rainy days. Horizontal rain is a common occurrence so rain pants are often necessary to remain dry and comfortable even when walking the city streets.

CITIES WITH SIMILAR CLIMATE: Craig, Thorne Bay, Metlakatla.

BUG INDEX: Insects aren't much of a problem within the city boundaries of Ketchikan, but exist at moderate to high levels in surrounding areas from May through September.

Monthly Summaries	JAN	FEB	MAR	APR	MAY	JUN
normal max. temp. F°	38.8	42.2	44.5	50.3	56.7	61.6
normal min. temp. F°	27.9	31.4	32.5	36.2	41.5	47.1
total precipitation (in.)	12.76	13.02	10.74	11.29	9.24	7.38
monthly snowfall (in.)	13.3	8.9	3.4	0.3	0.1	0.0
daylight on 15th	7:45	9:44	11:50	14:10	16:14	17:26

Alaskan Destinations 55

AURORA INDEX: Ketchikan's southern location makes Aurora viewing fair at best, and then only in the peak viewing seasons of fall and spring.

"Ketchikan Sneakers" are actually knee-high rubber boots. The term was phrased because everyone there wears rubber boots as their go-everywhere footwear in order to stay dry in Ketchikan's wet climate. So bring boots and rainwear if you want to be comfortable in this Southeast town. But, the fishing is great.

Monthly Summaries	JUL	AUG	SEP	OCT	NOV	DEC
normal max. temp. F°	65.3	65.4	60.4	52.0	44.9	40.8
normal min. temp. F°	51.0	51.6	47.2	40.9	34.6	31.1
total precipitation (in.)	7.12	10.55	13.73	22.43	16.92	15.47
monthly snowfall (in.)	0.0	0.0	0.0	0.1	2.3	8.6
daylight on 15th	16:52	15:00	12:44	10:29	8:20	7:08

KING SALMON

King Salmon is located a short distance inland from Bristol Bay at the beginning of the Alaska Peninsula. It lies in a great expanse of treeless, rolling tundra with no natural windbreaks. Its climate is predominated by wind, rain and mild temperatures.

Summer high temperatures average about 60° F with lows in the 40's. Occasional summer daytime highs will be above 70°. Temperatures are moderated by the average yearly cloud cover of eight-tenths of the sky. There is only about one clear day per summer month, which leaves about 29 days with some cloud cover.

Winter temperatures are relatively cold for a maritime location. This is due to the influence of cold air moving southwesterly from the Alaska mainland. October through April have daily minimums below freezing.

King Salmon averages about 150 days per year with a measurable amount of precipitation. Moist air coming northeasterly from Bristol Bay produces most of this. The yearly total precipitation is only about 20 inches which means it comes often, but in small amounts. Even so,

Monthly Summaries	JAN	FEB	MAR	APR	MAY	JUN
normal max. temp. F°	22.1	22.9	30.7	39.0	50.9	58.6
normal min. temp. F°	7.69	6.7	14.1	23.4	33.9	41.4
clear days	7.5	7.5	7.4	3.8	2.5	1.1
partly cloudy days	5.2	5.0	5.6	6.4	6.0	5.2
cloudy days	18.3	15.8	18.0	19.7	22.5	23.7
precipitation days	10.8	9.4	11.0	10.5	12.3	13.1
total precipitation (in.)	1.05	0.81	1.07	1.13	1.34	1.58
monthly snowfall (in.)	8.3	6.8	7.4	4.5	0.9	0.0
4 p.m. relative humidity	76	71	67	62	57	59
average wind speed	10.6	11.2	11.5	11.0	11.2	10.8
daylight on 15th	7:05	9:24	11:58	14:29	16:53	18:22

Alaskan Destinations 57

the fairly constant wind often produces horizontal rain or snow, which is much more bothersome than the typical vertical variety. Visitors to King Salmon would be well-advised to have good, head-to-toe raingear with them and always have it close at hand.

Snowfall in King Salmon averages about 45 inches, but the total accumulation is not nearly that deep, partly because some of it is wet and melts and mostly because of regular high winter winds which compact and move the snow. King Salmon often receives high winds from December through March with gusts of over 50 mph common and much higher speeds expected each year.

CITIES WITH SIMILAR CLIMATE: Naknek, Dillingham, Togiak.

BUG INDEX: High levels of biting insects all summer long despite the wind.

AURORA INDEX: Good viewing opportunities from fall to spring especially during the clear nights of winter.

Monthly Summaries	JUL	AUG	SEP	OCT	NOV	DEC
normal max. temp. F°	63.0	61.4	54.7	39.7	29.6	23.4
normal min. temp. F°	46.4	46.4	39.7	25.1	15.0	8.3
clear days	1.1	1.1	1.7	4.2	6.0	6.4
partly cloudy days	4.8	5.2	5.9	7.0	5.2	5.6
cloudy days	25.1	24.7	22.4	19.8	18.9	19.0
precipitation days	14.6	17.2	16.5	13.5	11.9	12.3
total precipitation (in.)	2.23	2.95	2.74	2.07	1.48	1.37
monthly snowfall (in.)	0.0	0.0	0.0	3.0	6.3	9.1
4 p.m. relative humidity	64	67	66	69	77	77
average wind speed	9.9	10.2	10.7	10.4	10.6	10.5
daylight on 15th	17:39	15:24	12:48	10:15	7:46	6:19

58
KODIAK

Kodiak is situated on the northeast end of Kodiak Island located in the Gulf of Alaska. It has a wet, windy climate typical of the maritime influences from the northern Pacific Ocean. Kodiak's marine influence is apparent in the limited range of both daily and annual temperatures.

Summer high temperatures average above 60° F only during July and August, with daily lows ranging only about a dozen degrees lower. By Alaskan standards it has a fair number of clear and partly cloudy days with only three months averaging over 20 cloudy days. Kodiak's proximity to the Gulf of Alaska is more of a factor than sunshine in determining the high range of summer temperatures.

Winter temperatures are mild. Although there are six months each winter with average minimums below freezing, the lowest average is only about 25° F. And the maximums for these six months are all above 35° F.

Kodiak receives about 65 inches of precipitation per year, and it is pretty well dispersed throughout the 12 months. Eight months of the

Monthly Summaries	JAN	FEB	MAR	APR	MAY	JUN
normal max. temp. F°	35.0	36.1	38.9	43.7	49.5	55.6
normal min. temp. F°	24.7	24.9	26.9	31.4	37.5	43.6
clear days	5.3	6.0	6.4	4.4	3.2	3.4
partly cloudy days	5.7	4.6	6.5	6.1	5.5	5.7
cloudy days	20.0	17.6	18.0	19.5	22.3	20.9
precipitation days	17.2	15.9	16.5	16.1	17.8	15.3
total precipitation (in.)	7.38	5.28	4.63	4.20	5.52	4.78
monthly snowfall (in.)	15.4	17.8	13.0	8.0	0.7	T
4 p.m. relative humidity	76	73	69	69	73	75
average wind speed	12.7	12.5	12.5	11.6	10.7	9.3
daylight on 15th	7:15	9:27	11:45	14:20	16:38	18:03

Alaskan Destinations 59

year average a measurable amount of snow, although most of it doesn't persist throughout winter. Rain comes in measurable amounts over 15 days per month, spring through fall.

Wind speed is quite variable in Kodiak with frequent strong winds making the daily average of over 11 mph slightly misleading. In reality, slightly breezy and even windless days are quite common, especially in summer. The stronger winds are much more commonly associated with winter storms. Very strong gusts of over 120 mph have been measured near the town site.

CITIES WITH SIMILAR CLIMATE: Port Lions, Karluk.

BUG INDEX: Moderate levels of insects near town during summer months. Outlying areas on the island can have high levels from late May through September.

AURORA INDEX: Fair viewing opportunities during late fall and early spring months.

Monthly Summaries	JUL	AUG	SEP	OCT	NOV	DEC
normal max. temp. F°	60.5	61.9	56.6	47.2	39.9	36.4
normal min. temp. F°	48.2	48.4	43.4	34.2	28.8	25.2
clear days	3.1	4.2	4.0	5.8	7.0	6.0
partly cloudy days	5.6	7.0	7.4	7.7	6.6	5.6
cloudy days	22.3	19.8	18.6	17.4	16.4	19.4
precipitation days	14.7	14.2	15.8	16.3	16.4	17.5
total precipitation (in.)	3.7	5.15	6.99	7.18	5.96	6.81
monthly snowfall (in.)	0.0	0.0	0.0	2.3	7.7	13.2
4 p.m. relative humidity	77	74	73	69	72	74
average wind speed	7.7	8.4	9.7	11.4	12.6	12.6
daylight on 15th	17:27	15:21	12:51	10:23	7:59	6:34

60
MCGRATH

McGrath is located in the western interior of Alaska on the upper Kuskokwim River. Its climate is similar in many ways to that of Fairbanks, about 250 miles farther inland. McGrath is not quite as warm in summer, just as cold in winter and has noticeably more precipitation than Fairbanks.

Summer maximum temperatures average in the mid to upper 60's with over fifteen days over 80° F each summer. As in most Alaskan cities, evenings are typically cool, but the average breezes are light which makes for (slightly) more comfortable conditions.

Winter lows are quite cold with November through March having average minimums below zero. Extreme lows of -50° F are expected each winter. Extended periods of ten or more days of extreme cold are common. Blankets of ice-fog enveloping the town commonly accompany these cold snaps. The transition seasons are short however, so spring and fall come and go quickly. The result is that summer temperatures return quickly in May and last through mid-September.

Monthly Summaries	JAN	FEB	MAR	APR	MAY	JUN
normal max. temp. F°	0.4	8.9	23.4	37.0	54.5	65.5
normal min. temp. F°	-17.8	-14.2	-2.9	16.0	34.5	45.1
clear days	9.2	9.0	9.1	7.3	4.0	1.8
partly cloudy days	4.8	4.4	6.2	7.2	8.3	8.7
cloudy days	17.0	14.8	15.7	15.6	18.7	19.5
precipitation days	9.7	8.3	9.2	7.1	9.5	12.7
total precipitation (in.)	0.75	0.66	0.80	0.82	0.87	1.47
monthly snowfall (in.)	14.4	12.0	12.4	6.9	0.9	0.0
4 p.m. relative humidity	71	63	53	49	44	48
average wind speed	3.2	4.4	5.3	6.5	6.7	6.4
daylight on 15th	5:50	8:48	11:41	14:53	17:58	20:13

Alaskan Destinations   61

Precipitation is only about 15 inches per year in McGrath, but 40 percent of that comes in July, August and September. Even so, McGrath averages over 90 inches of snow per year and most of that persists all winter. Alaska's typically dry snow explains the high snowfall, yet low total precipitation levels in winter. (Ten to twenty inches of Alaska snow has the water equivalent of only about one inch.) There are occasional thaws during winter when warm southerly winds reach McGrath from the Gulf of Alaska.

The Kuskokwim River typically breaks up around mid-May, and the ground thaws around the end of the month. McGrath has a 120-day growing season and, given the high temperatures and long daylight hours, could support some great vegetable farms. However, its remote location and lack of people (population around 550) have prevented commercial agriculture operations.

BUG INDEX: Very high in summer months, both in town and nearby areas.

AURORA INDEX: Very good viewing possibilities for the Aurora from fall through spring.

Monthly Summaries	JUL	AUG	SEP	OCT	NOV	DEC
normal max. temp. F°	68.4	63.5	52.9	31.3	12.4	2.7
normal min. temp. F°	49.0	45.0	35.4	18.0	-3.7	-14.6
clear days	2.2	2.3	3.5	3.8	6.4	7.6
partly cloudy days	7.7	5.3	4.9	4.8	4.4	4.5
cloudy days	21.1	23.4	21.6	22.4	19.2	18.9
precipitation days	14.7	17.2	13.9	12.4	11.7	11.9
total precipitation (in.)	2.05	2.47	1.98	1.40	1.29	1.40
monthly snowfall (in.)	T	T	1.1	10.2	17.1	18.7
4 p.m. relative humidity	55	61	61	69	75	74
average wind speed	6.0	5.8	5.9	5.4	3.8	3.2
daylight on 15th	18:11	16:12	13:02	9:59	6:53	4:49

MCKINLEY PARK

McKinley Park is located within the Alaska Range in the interior portion of the state. The town of McKinley Park is just on the edge of the boundary of Denali National Park (previously called McKinley National Park) overlooking the Nenana River. (The following data has all been recorded at the town site.) The town and Park has cool, wet summers and moderately cold winters. There are approximately 200 year-round residents in the town.

Summer average maximum temperatures are in the mid 60's. Daily temperatures occasionally top 80° F. The highest recorded summer temperature at the town site is 91° F on July 22, 1991. The average summer minimums are around 40° F. The lowest recorded summer temperature is 17° F on August 31, 1987.

Winter maximum temperatures average in the low teens. The average minimums for the nine month period from September through May are all below freezing. The coldest recorded temperature is -54° F on February 5, 1999.

Yearly precipitation at the town site is about 15 inches. Over 50 percent of this total falls during June, July and August. The yearly snowfall averages over 80 inches and most of that persists all winter. All months except July and August have measurable snowfall in an average year. The heaviest monthly snowfall on record is 98 inches in March, 1948.

Situated as it is on a narrow river valley within some of the highest mountains in North America, the town site experiences year-round windy conditions. Although winter is more prone to gusty winds of storm intensities, summer winds often reach 15 mph,

Monthly Summaries	JAN	FEB	MAR	APR	MAY	JUN
normal max. temp. F°	10.1	14.4	25.7	38.0	53.6	63.6
normal min. temp. F°	-7.9	-6.1	0.7	14.5	28.8	38.6
total precipitation (in.)	0.70	0.51	0.57	0.38	0.80	2.47
monthly snowfall (in.)	10.5	9.4	7.9	6.5	2.6	0.3
daylight on 15th	6:03	9:01	11:45	15:21	18:30	20:51

Alaskan Destinations 63

making jackets mandatory for comfort during any outdoor activity. The best choice of jackets would be a waterproof variety–preferably made of a waterproof-yet-breathable material. These can be worn as windbreakers when it isn't raining without excessive moisture gathering inside to make the wearer damp. The characteristic light rains of this area are seldom wet enough to pass through this type of jacket even after many hours of exposure. Using a completely waterproof variety would only result in more body moisture staying inside, which would make the wearer uncomfortable.

Light hats and gloves are also recommended for visitors. These should be stuffed in ample coat pockets to be readily available when needed. They will often make the difference between comfort and a slow loss of body heat resulting in getting thoroughly chilled. When this happens, the wonderful experience of Denali is seriously compromised. Planning ahead will ensure your trip will be as enjoyable as possible.

CITIES WITH SIMILAR CLIMATE: Cantwell, Healy, Anderson.

BUG INDEX: Although windy conditions help keep the insects from attacking visitors, anytime the wind lets up or is blocked by an obstruction they can be found at high levels during all summer months. This applies to the town site as well as the National Park.

AURORA INDEX: Good viewing possibilities anytime the night sky is at least partly clear from late fall until early spring. During summer the long daylight hours and residual light pollution all night long makes viewing possibilities very poor.

Monthly Summaries	JUL	AUG	SEP	OCT	NOV	DEC
normal max. temp. F°	66.8	62.0	51.1	31.8	16.8	11.7
normal min. temp. F°	42.2	38.9	30.0	13.2	-0.8	-5.8
total precipitation (in.)	3.19	2.41	1.57	1.06	0.94	0.90
monthly snowfall (in.)	0.0	0.0	4.1	14.4	12.5	13.9
daylight on 15th	19:34	16:26	13:01	9:46	6:30	4:11

NOME

Nome is located on the south side of the Seward Peninsula on the western border of Alaska. Its climate displays a significant maritime affect from Norton Sound which lies immediately to the south. The town is bordered by treeless tundra on the north.

Summer maximum temperatures average only into the high 50's–partly because of its northern latitude and partly because of the moderating affect of Norton Sound. June, July and August have all recorded occasional days into the low 80's. Every month of the year has also recorded occasional days below the freezing mark.

Winter temperatures are moderated somewhat by nearby Norton Sound, but winter winds can be fierce without any barriers to protect the town both from winds off the water and cold continental winds from the Northeast. Although ambient winter temperatures are not terribly extreme, daily minimums are below freezing from early October until early May–half of the year.

Visitors who travel to Nome to view the finish of "The Last Great Race"—the Iditarod—need to bring complete arctic gear to

Monthly Summaries	JAN	FEB	MAR	APR	MAY	JUN
normal max. temp. F°	14.7	12.2	17.4	25..5	42.0	52.9
normal min. temp. F°	-0.7	-4.5	-0.3	9.7	29.2	38.8
clear days	10.1	11.6	11.2	9.2	7.2	5.9
partly cloudy days	4.3	3.6	5.1	6.2	7.6	8.9
cloudy days	16.6	13.1	14.6	14.6	16.2	15.3
precipitation days	10.9	8.2	9.5	8.8	8.1	8.9
total precipitation (in.)	0.79	0.60	0.54	0.68	0.62	1.12
monthly snowfall (in.)	9.2	6.5	7.5	6.6	2.2	0.1
4 p.m. relative humidity	74	71	70	74	73	73
average wind speed	11.2	10.8	10.2	10.2	10.0	9.7
daylight on 15th	5:15	8:33	11:40	15:06	18:31	21:22

Alaskan Destinations 65

survive the weather. Mid-March still finds Nome wrapped up tightly in the depths of winter weather with subzero temperatures for at least part of the day coupled with frigid winds. However, the end of the Iditarod almost coincides with the spring equinox, so there are almost 12 hours of daylight at this time–making it slightly more hospitable than earlier in the winter.

Precipitation is moderate in Nome even though it is located seaside. The annual total is less than 15 inches per year. About half of that total comes in July, August and September. December through May each produce less than one inch. Blizzards are common especially in early winter–November and December.

CITIES WITH SIMILAR CLIMATE: Kotzebue, Unalakleet.

BUG INDEX: Insects can be horrendous in summer months and barely survivable with the best protection–headnets, gloves and thick, tightly closed clothing.

AURORA INDEX: Excellent viewing can be had from Nome during much of the winter–of course this is always dependant on if the Aurora happens to be displaying on a given evening and if the cloud cover allows for good visibility.

Monthly Summaries	JUL	AUG	SEP	OCT	NOV	DEC
normal max. temp. F°	57.7	56.1	48.7	33.7	22.5	15.1
normal min. temp. F°	45.2	44.1	36.3	22.2	9.3	-0.5
clear days	3.9	2.9	4.7	7.0	7.6	10.0
partly cloudy days	6.8	5.8	5.6	5.5	4.3	3.9
cloudy days	20.2	22.3	19.7	18.4	18.2	17.1
precipitation days	12.5	15.7	13.9	10.8	12.1	10.4
total precipitation (in.)	2.17	2.71	2.43	1.35	1.04	0.83
monthly snowfall (in.)	0.0	0.0	0.5	4.6	10.8	9.4
4 p.m. relative humidity	78	79	73	72	75	74
average wind speed	9.7	10.4	11.0	10.7	11.6	10.4
daylight on 15th	19:57	16:32	13:06	9:50	6:26	4:00

PALMER

Palmer is located in Southcentral Alaska within the Matanuska-Susitna Valley. Palmer's sister city, Wasilla, is just ten miles west and Anchorage lies about 30 miles to the southwest. Palmer (as well as Wasilla) enjoys a mild climate due to the influence of nearby Knik Arm–an extension of Cook Inlet. Winters are not terribly harsh and summers are pleasant.

Summer high temperatures average in the low 60's for June, July and August. The temperature does rise into the 70's several times each summer and occasionally it does reach 80° F. Afternoon thundershowers and lightning displays are more and more common in many areas around Palmer since the 1980's. Nights are cool with low's averaging just above 40° F.

Winter temperatures are below freezing from mid-October through the end of March. Winter low averages seldom go below the zero mark. However, occasional cold spells will drive the daily lows to -20 or -30° F for several days at a time.

Strong, gusty winds often occur during all months of the year in and near Palmer. The town sits at the conjunction of the Matanuska and Knik Rivers and receives high winds funneling down both of these drainages. The winds often carry a lot of glacial dust and can create dust clouds which can be seen for miles and sometimes even block the sunlight for part of the day.

Palmer only gets about 12 inches of rain per year and 40 inches of snow. Because of the windy conditions in winter, there is seldom more than a 12 inch accumulation of snow at any time in town, although nearby, protected areas may have two or three times

Monthly Summaries	JAN	FEB	MAR	APR	MAY	JUN
normal max. temp. F°	12.1	17.0	24.2	37.8	51.5	61.2
normal min. temp. F°	-0.6	2.8	7.0	19.2	30.9	40.1
total precipitation (in.)	0.4	0.9	0.7	1.1	0.7	2.2
monthly snowfall (in.)	5.2	6.3	2.9	2.3	0.3	0.0
daylight on 15th	6:19	9:04	11:46	14:58	16:37	19:30

Alaskan Destinations 67

that much. The rainiest months in town are June and July. However, weather near Palmer can vary greatly because of the abrupt changes in topography as the two river valleys meet. Nearby mountainsides often get twice the rainfall as Palmer and the timing is usually later in the summer.

CITIES WITH SIMILAR CLIMATE: Wasilla, Houston, Chickaloon.

BUG INDEX: Moderate levels of insect activity in summer months.

AURORA INDEX: Good viewing possibilities from late fall to early spring.

These two hikers have reached the top of Bodenburg Butte, near Palmer. Unexpected winds coming off the nearby glaciers or mountains can suddenly make a warm day uncomfortable, unless you plan ahead by bringing a windproof, waterproof coat– like each of these climbers is wearing.

Monthly Summaries	JUL	AUG	SEP	OCT	NOV	DEC
normal max. temp. F°	63.2	60.6	50.9	33.9	19.1	10.9
normal min. temp. F°	43.0	40.9	33.0	18.9	6.2	-0.9
total precipitation (in.)	2.5	1.2	1.1	0.9	0.6	0.7
monthly snowfall (in.)	0.0	0.0	0.7	8.5	6.6	8.5
daylight on 15th	18:34	15:52	12:55	10:01	7:09	5:22

68
PRUDHOE BAY

Prudhoe Bay sits on Alaska's northern coast on the edge of the Arctic Ocean. This "town" was created as a temporary residence for workers in the nearby oil fields. Its climate is arctic with cool summers, cold winters and short transition seasons between the two.

July and August are the only months which have average high temperatures over 50° F. The average summer lows are all below 40° F. Nonetheless, when conditions are right with 24-hour-long, clear days and little wind, the tundra expanses surrounding Prudhoe Bay can be downright hot at times. The heat, plus the intense bug activity as insects try to cram a year's worth of living into a few short months, can make this arctic environment uncomfortable for humans. Understandably, few people try to live in this area.

By the end of September, summer has passed and winter freeze-up begins. Winter temperatures aren't as low as places inland from the Arctic Ocean, but January's average high is still below -11° F. Daily averages above freezing don't return until late May or early June–depending on the year.

Precipitation for the year totals less than 5 inches. The small amount of moisture which does fall to the ground remains there for a long while. In places, the tundra is actually boggy in summer. Winter snows are light, but they, too, persist for a long time. Blizzards move the snow around during winter making whiteout conditions another hindrance to man's survival, but the scant snow is just moved back and forth and not actually removed from the environment.

Monthly Summaries	JAN	FEB	MAR	APR	MAY	JUN
normal max. temp. F°	-11.7	-9.7	-4.7	10.7	28.8	45.2
normal min. temp. F°	-23.6	-24.1	-20.0	-4.5	18.8	32.7
total precipitation (in.)	0.2	0.2	0.1	0.1	0.1	0.4
monthly snowfall (in.)	2.8	2.4	2.6	1.7	1.3	1.1
daylight on 15th	0:00	7:15	11:32	16:12	22:40	24:00

Alaskan Destinations 69

Winds coming off the Arctic Ocean in summer and from inland in winter add to Prudhoe's reputation as a cold place to visit. Although the winds aren't generally strong by Alaskan standards, they do make the chill factor an important consideration when planning a trip to this northern destination.

BUG INDEX: Once the summer warms up in mid-June, the insect activity can be frightening. Local lore claims that without clothing for protection, a man would soon die from loss of blood to the clouds of bloodsucking insects.

AURORA INDEX: Fair to good viewing opportunities for the Aurora when cloud cover and ice fog don't obstruct the view. The Aurora's center is actually south of Prudhoe Bay.

The Prudhoe Bay landscape is barren tundra except for man-made structures like this drilling rig. Situated on the Arctic Ocean, the weather here is usually cool or cold. Dress warmly.

Monthly Summaries	JUL	AUG	SEP	OCT	NOV	DEC
normal max. temp. F°	55.4	51	38.3	20.6	-0.2	-7.4
normal min. temp. F°	39.7	37.5	28.9	9.1	-12.2	-19.8
total precipitation (in.)	0.7	1.1	0.6	0.4	0.2	0.2
monthly snowfall (in.)	0.0	0.5	3.5	10	4.5	3.3
daylight on 15th	24:00	18:22	13:27	9:04	3:41	0:00

SITKA

Sitka is located in Southeast Alaska on Baranof Island. Its environment is best characterized as being a northern rain forest. Sitka and Ketchikan are often referred to as being in Alaska's "Banana Belt" because of their uncharacteristically warm climates. Sitka's monthly average temperatures are above freezing for all months of the year. There are winter cold snaps when it actually stays below freezing for days at a time, but these are usually of short duration.

Although it doesn't really get "Alaska" cold in winter, Sitka also doesn't get very warm in summer. Summer high temperatures average barely above 60° F for only two months a year. The nearby Pacific Ocean is the main reason for these cool summers.

Winter high temperatures average around 40° F, only seven or eight degrees lower than what you would find in Seattle, Washington at that time of year. The damp, foggy climate is also similar to Seattle, so appropriate dress can be determined by planning for the colder extremes of Seattle.

Steady winds are common in Sitka because of its proximity to the ocean. Warm summer temperatures can quickly turn chilling if a stiff wind comes up–which it frequently does in this seaside destination. Storm force winds also arise frequently in both summer and winter with uncomfortably strong gusts. Dressing to withstand these winds will allow visitors to move around outdoors in acceptable comfort for short durations. Otherwise, visitors may stay indoors or on board and miss their chance to visit this town.

Precipitation averages about 86 inches annually. June and July are actually the driest months of the year with about 4 inches each month, with levels increasing in August and peaking at over 13

Monthly Summaries	JAN	FEB	MAR	APR	MAY	JUN
normal max. temp. F°	38.1	40.7	43.0	47.7	53.2	57.4
normal min. temp. F°	30.0	31.6	33.1	36.0	41.2	46.7
total precipitation (in.)	8.06	6.19	6.02	5.00	4.64	3.87
daylight on 15th	7:24	9:30	11:46	14:16	16:30	17:52

Alaskan Destinations 71

inches in October. The snow which does fall during winter is almost always wet and doesn't last more than a week or so.

BUG INDEX: Low levels in the business districts of town, but moderate to high levels in outlying areas during summer months.

AURORA INDEX: Fair viewing opportunities at best during the peak of Aurora activity–late fall and early spring. The southern location and cloud cover both hamper viewing.

The bays, fiords, passages and other waterways around Sitka can be breathtakingly beautiful when the sun shines. These fisherman knows how just how fickle the weather in Southeast can be as they are wearing raingear even on a sunny day–just in case.

Monthly Summaries	JUL	AUG	SEP	OCT	NOV	DEC
normal max. temp. F°	61.0	62.1	58.3	50.5	42.8	39.3
normal min. temp. F°	51.1	51.9	47.9	41.7	34.6	31.7
total precipitation (in.)	4.02	6.58	10.90	13.96	8.78	8.05
daylight on 15th	17:17	15:16	12:50	10:26	8:07	6:45

72
TALKEETNA

Talkeetna is about 80 air miles north of Anchorage in Southcentral Alaska. The town sits on the southern bank of the Talkeetna River where it joins the Susitna River. The climate is continental with a maritime influence from the not-too-distant Gulf of Alaska, 150 miles to the south.

Summer maximum temperatures average in the mid to high 60's with occasional days reaching 80° F. Daily lows are usually in the 40's with freeze-free dates averaging only from mid-June to mid-August. The continental influence is exhibited in this short growing season. Summer cloud cover is relatively light for Alaskan towns, reflecting the remoteness from any large body of water.

Winter temperatures can stay below zero for (unusual) short periods up to a few weeks, but the average lows are not below zero for any month of the year. Winter daily maximums are almost 20° F for the coldest months of December and January.

Monthly Summaries	JAN	FEB	MAR	APR	MAY	JUN
normal max. temp. F°	19.2	25.4	33.4	43.4	56.0	64.4
normal min. temp. F°	0.6	4.0	9.8	22.4	33.8	44.4
clear days	5.8	8.2	9.4	5.0	6.0	1.0
partly cloudy days	4.0	3.7	4.0	5.0	6.0	12.0
cloudy days	21.0	15.9	17.6	18.3	19.0	17.0
precipitation days	9.1	8.7	9.0	7.2	11.7	12.8
total precipitation (in.)	1.30	1.44	1.46	1.59	1.67	2.63
monthly snowfall (in.)	20.0	18.5	17.8	7.9	0.8	T
4 p.m. relative humidity	69	64	59	52	50	54
average wind speed	6.3	5.7	5.4	4.8	5.0	5.3
daylight on 15th	6:06	8:58	11:46	14:53	17:50	19:52

Alaskan Destinations 73

The highest frequency and quantity of precipitation comes mostly in August and September–typical of most Alaska locales. Talkeetna receives over 110 inches of snow annually and almost 30 inches of total precipitation. Like many Alaska towns, there are usually a few thaws during winter which reduce the level of snow accumulation.

Winds are light in Talkeetna with few occurrences of strong windstorms.

BUG INDEX: Moderate levels in town because there is little pavement or concrete. Higher levels near the river or just out of town.

AURORA INDEX: Good viewing possibilities all winter long.

Monthly Summaries	JUL	AUG	SEP	OCT	NOV	DEC
normal max. temp. F°	67.7	64.5	55.6	39.3	25.2	17.7
normal min. temp. F°	49.0	45.7	36.6	23.1	7.9	2.9
clear days	5.0	3.0	5.1	5.9	7.5	5.4
partly cloudy days	7.0	11.0	4.3	4.9	3.4	2.3
cloudy days	19.0	17.0	18.8	19.7	19.0	22.5
precipitation days	14.7	16.4	16.0	13.1	10.4	11.5
total precipitation (in.)	3.63	4.52	4.23	3.10	1.73	1.91
monthly snowfall (in.)	0.0	T	0.2	10.3	17.3	21.9
4 p.m. relative humidity	61	64	64	68	72	73
average wind speed	4.3	3.8	3.8	3.8	5.2	5.1
daylight on 15th	18:51	16:00	12:56	9:57	6:59	5:05

74
VALDEZ

Valdez sits at the head of Valdez Arm, an extension of Prince William Sound. The terminus of the Alaska Oil Pipeline is across the Arm a few miles from town. The town is nestled on a small glacial plain at the water's edge flanked by steep, forested, rugged peaks of the Chugach Mountains. The climate is cool, cloudy, wet and snowy.

Summer high temperatures average in the low 60's with a few days each summer over 70° F. Occasional temperatures as high as 80° F have been recorded. The close proximity of the ocean and steep, glaciated mountains keeps the temperatures cool.

Winter temperatures are barely below freezing although cold spells of several days with minimums around zero can occur. Daytime highs are not below freezing until mid-November and climb back above 32° F by mid-March–a relatively short winter by Alaskan standards.

Precipitation is high, both in summer and winter. Every month of the year averages over 15 days of precipitation. The driest months

Monthly Summaries	JAN	FEB	MAR	APR	MAY	JUN
normal max. temp. F°	25.9	30.0	35.9	44.2	52.5	59.1
normal min. temp. F°	15.0	18.1	22.4	22.9	37.8	44.4
clear days	5.4	6.5	7.4	5.8	3.6	2.9
partly cloudy days	3.5	2.7	3.5	5.0	5.1	5.3
cloudy days	22.1	19.1	20.1	19.2	22.3	21.8
precipitation days	17.0	14.2	15.8	14.1	16.7	15.3
total precipitation (in.)	5.6	5.13	4.70	3.16	3.83	3.08
monthly snowfall (in.)	65.4	57.4	54.3	21.7	0.6	0.0
4 p.m. relative humidity	75	68	66	62	63	65
average wind speed	7.2	8.2	6.5	5.1	5.7	5.8
daylight on 15th	6:28	9:07	11:47	14:44	17:29	19:17

Alaskan Destinations 75

are April through July and the wettest are September and October. An average of 64 inches of precipitation falls each year. Valdez boasts Alaska's **highest average annual snowfall of 329 inches**. It is not surprising that the state record for the largest single snowfall—62 inches— and the largest monthly snowfall—297 inches— occurred just north of Valdez in Thompson Pass.

Winds are generally light during summer, but winter pressure gradients can produce very high winds coming through nearby passes. However, anyone planning to be out on Valdez Arm, even in summer, should realize that stronger winds are much more common on the water and should be prepared with warm, wind-resistant clothing.

CITIES WITH SIMILAR CLIMATE: Seward, Cordova and Whittier are other towns in Prince William Sound with similar climates, but are slightly warmer and have a little less snow than Valdez.

BUG INDEX: Moderate levels in summer.

AURORA INDEX: Only fair viewing opportunities because of heavy cloud cover in fall and spring.

Monthly Summaries	JUL	AUG	SEP	OCT	NOV	DEC
normal max. temp. F°	62.3	60.8	54.1	43.4	32.4	27.8
normal min. temp. F°	47.5	46.2	40.4	32.7	22.4	18.0
clear days	3.5	4.4	3.5	4.7	6.2	5.1
partly cloudy days	4.3	5.3	4.5	2.9	3.8	1.9
cloudy days	23.2	21.3	22.0	23.4	20.0	24.0
precipitation days	17.0	17.0	20.4	19.9	15.3	18.0
total precipitation (in.)	3.84	5.96	8.37	8.07	5.50	6.80
monthly snowfall (in.)	0.0	0.0	0.2	10.5	42.1	76.2
4 p.m. relative humidity	71	72	74	72	69	76
average wind speed	4.9	4.2	4.4	6.2	8.2	6.7
daylight on 15th	18:24	15:47	12:53	10:04	7:16	5:33

76
WRANGELL

Wrangell is located in Southeast Alaska on Wrangell Island. It sits on the Alaska Marine Highway route and is one of the many little towns adorning the Inside Passageway of Southeast Alaska. Wrangell has a wet, cool climate with mild winters.

Summer temperatures in Wrangell average in the low 60's for daytime highs and the upper 40's for evening lows. Clear days will often produce temperatures into the mid-70's, but rarely over the 80° F mark.

Winter daytime temperatures all average over the freezing mark. The ocean's influence keeps even the lows from seldom dropping below 10° F. Although there is an annual average of 54 inches of snow, the average snow depth is less than 4 inches for any winter month. Above-freezing temperatures melt most of the winter's snows within a few weeks.

Precipitation during summer is lowest in June and July, with 4.6 and 5.6 inches, respectively. Increasing amounts in September lead to the wettest month in October–with over 12 inches of rain. Overcast skies and rain are normal conditions in most southeastern towns, and Wrangell is no exception.

Like most seaside towns in Alaska, Wrangell has its share of wind. Sea breezes are daily occurrences and stronger gusts of 20 to 30 mph are weekly expectations. Rain often travels sideways so visitors should be prepared with waterproof, or at least water-resistant clothing from head to toe if they expect to remain comfortable during any extended outdoor experience.

Monthly Summaries	JAN	FEB	MAR	APR	MAY	JUN
normal max. temp. F°	33.1	37.6	42.2	49.1	56.3	61.8
normal min. temp. F°	23.5	27.2	30.6	35.1	40.6	46.0
total precipitation (in.)	6.39	5.73	5.22	4.70	4.38	3.96
monthly snowfall (in.)	17.8	11.9	6.9	0.8	0.0	0.0
daylight on 15th	7:33	9:37	11:50	14:16	16:26	17:43

Alaskan Destinations 77

CITIES WITH SIMILAR CLIMATE: Petersburg.

BUG INDEX: Moderate levels from May through September, with the most abundance from late June through early August.

AURORA INDEX: Fair viewing in late fall and early spring, when cloud cover doesn't interfere.

The waters around Wrangell abound with fish of all shapes and sizes. This 100 lb. halibut will make many good meals for this lucky fisherman who was able to take his raingear off for the photo. Southeast Alaska weather is wet year-round, so you should never be far from rainproof clothing.

Monthly Summaries	JUL	AUG	SEP	OCT	NOV	DEC
normal max. temp. F°	64.4	63.7	57.9	49.5	41.1	36.2
normal min. temp. F°	49.4	49.3	45.4	38.7	31.6	27.1
total precipitation (in.)	4.63	5.63	9.04	12.84	8.94	7.96
monthly snowfall (in.)	0.0	0.0	0.0	0.1	4.8	12.4
daylight on 15th	17:06	15:08	12:46	10:25	8:10	6:53

Because of the sheer size of Alaska, visitors may experience a wide range of weather extremes–depending on their choice of destination(s). Studying the long-term weather patterns (climate) of your destination(s) is the first step toward successful wardrobe planning for an Alaskan visit. The next step is to understand how the new millennium's clothing, footwear and other gear is designed to keep you warm, dry and comfortable.

This North Face Mountain Light coat is made with a layer of semipermeable GoreTex to keep you dry and comfortable in wind, rain or just cool temperatures all day without feeling clammy. Wearing non-breathable raingear all day will sometimes chill you because of moisture buildup on the inside.

CHAPTER THREE

CLOTHING SELECTION GUIDELINES

There is a tremendous variety of clothing designed specifically for outdoor use. Much of this clothing can be used effectively in Alaska depending on the destination and the season. A good understanding of the function and design of clothing is a prerequisite to making sensible choices between the hundreds of brands, styles and fabrics available. Knowing how to select the best outdoor clothing and when to use each garment will help you enjoy your Alaskan experience.

HEAT TRANSFER & RETENTION

Clothing keeps us warm because it slows down heat transfer from our bodies to the environment, thus helping us retain our body heat. Understanding the physics of heat transfer and retention will help you make better clothing selections. The four ways we can lose heat from our bodies are convection, conduction, radiation and evaporation. *Convection* occurs when heat near your skin is removed by air currents. Clothing protects us from this form of heat loss to the extent that it (the clothing) is windproof. The stronger the wind and the colder the temperatures, the thicker and less porous the clothing must be to prevent convection heat loss.

Conduction heat loss occurs by body contact with cold items or substances. Leaning against a cold building, grabbing cold metal items, sitting on a cold boat seat, or being immersed in water are good examples of situations where conduction heat loss occurs rapidly. This is why sleeping on the ground without a sleeping pad is so cold. The cold ground drains our body heat. Conduction is also why we lose heat so quickly in cold water. Heat travels 30 times faster through water than air. A person has 30 minutes to 3 hours before dying of hypothermia in 40 to 60 degree Fahrenheit water. A person in 35 to 40 degree water only has 15 to 60 minutes to live; in 32 degree water you have less than 15 minutes to survive. Conduction heat loss also occurs to the air, but at a much slower rate than to dense objects or substances.

Radiation heat loss happens as our skin slowly gives out our body heat through the air. This is the heat you feel when you get close to a warm object without touching it. The majority of our bodies' heat loss by radiation is stopped if we are wearing even a light layer of clothing. Radiation is not usually a significant source of heat loss.

Walking on a glacier is a fascinating experience–you feel the surreal cooling effect (by conduction and convection) of millions of tons of ice beneath you and can even feel the "river of ice" move if you are lucky. Warm clothing will help make the experience an enjoyable one.

Clothing Selection Guidelines 81

Evaporation heat loss occurs when water evaporates, removing substantial amounts of heat as it does so. This is why being wet makes us feel so cold. The moisture on our skin or in our clothing is constantly evaporating and taking our body heat with it. This is also why wearing wet cotton clothing can be colder than wearing no clothing, but having dry skin. Wet cotton clothing has probably caused more hypothermia cases than just about any other factor. This method of heat loss is the reason staying dry is so critical to being comfortable in the often-wet weather of Alaska.

The major points about heat loss to remember are: 1) Remain as dry as possible, and wear nonabsorbent clothing which retains its insulating values even when damp. 2) Stay out of the wind as much as possible, and wear windproof clothing. Convection heat loss by moving air can be a substantial drain on body heat here in Alaska. Even with thick, windproof clothing we will still lose a lot of heat if our heads and faces are exposed to the wind. So seeking shelter from the wind is a high priority for retaining body heat.

HEAT RETENTION

Convection, conduction, radiation and evaporation are all ways we lose heat. One basic requirement of outdoor clothing is that it helps *retain* our body heat by slowing down heat loss through these four methods. To slow heat loss by *convection*, clothing should slow or stop wind currents from reaching the skin. Tightly woven fabrics or coated materials like rain wear are best for this. Clothing slows down *conduction* heat loss by trapping air between its fibers. Since air is a poor conductor, body heat is lost slowly through clothing which holds a lot of small air pockets. Wearing layers of clothing is another way to trap layers of air to slow the loss of body heat by conduction.

Radiation heat loss is not significantly affected by most types of clothing. However, shiny materials like those used in space blankets do depend on their ability to block radiation heat loss as part of their effectiveness. *Evaporation* heat loss is directly linked to the amount of moisture which clothing repels, absorbs, and/or holds against the skin. Slowing this type of heat loss is best accomplished by staying as dry as possible. This is the reason a top priority when choosing outdoor clothing for Alaska is how dry it will keep you.

Heat loss by evaporation is often the most significant factor in loss of body heat.

Comfortable clothing should not only keep a person warm and dry, but also cool them when necessary. In warm weather under a hot sun, the appropriate clothing will help dissipate body heat, yet be warm enough should the temperature drop suddenly. Clothing's comfort factor also depends on its feel on the skin. This is mostly personal preference–some people can't wear wool because it irritates their skin, others don't like synthetics and feel natural fabrics are intrinsically better. This is a factor which has to be determined by personal experience.

HYPOTHERMIA

Hypothermia is a gradual drop in body temperature which, if untreated, can lead to death. There are several casual Alaskan visitors who fall victim to hypothermia each year. It is not a topic reserved just for hard-core outdoor enthusiasts. Even seemingly safe activities like bus rides or boat tours can put people at risk if accidents, mechanical failures or sudden weather changes occur. A basic understanding about the causes and effects of hypothermia is useful wherever you travel or live.

Although hypothermia can be a threat to your well-being during almost any weather and in almost any climate, Alaska's wet, cool climate often provides the perfect conditions for hypothermia. Staying warm and dry on your visit are the two best ways to avoid becoming a victim.

Temperatures which most often cause hypothermia are around 40 to 50 degrees Fahrenheit. Because many people don't recognize the threat of hypothermia at these temperatures, they don't dress and act accordingly—whereas at below-freezing temperatures most people do recognize the danger, so their appropriate dress and actions help prevent hypothermia.

Other factors greatly increasing the chances of hypothermia are exhaustion and dehydration—conditions which tend to sneak up on people before they realize it. Alcohol consumption also predisposes a person to hypothermia, as does any other factor that prevents body heat generation from keeping pace with heat loss.

Clothing Selection Guidelines 83

Hypothermia is so dangerous because of its ability to strike at unexpected times. This July hike suddenly turned cool, wet and windy—prime hypothermia conditions—for these prepared hikers. Even though well-prepared, they were only able to stop briefly before heading back down to escape the "summer" weather.

Because this condition is not traumatic, but often a cumulative result of many hours of slow heat loss (usually from exposure in an outdoor situation), it can sneak up on the most experienced outdoor enthusiasts; which is another reason it is such a threat to everyone and one which has to be guarded against continually.

One of the best ways to guard against hypothermia is by choosing the right clothing. If the temperature is expected to drop below 60 degrees Fahrenheit during an activity or an unexpected night out due to an accident (and that includes just about any day in Alaska), visitors should consider hypothermia a real threat and plan accordingly. Wet cotton clothing can actually be worse than dry skin for insulating value. Cotton should only be worn when temperatures will not drop below 60 degrees Fahrenheit, the distance to shelter will always be short, reliable transportation is always available, or companions will always be nearby. Even then, I am very cautious of cotton because of the ever-present possibility of mishaps, especially injury, which—combined with wet weather—could still lead to hypothermia in the most unlikely situations.

It is much safer to wear wool or synthetic clothing during any outdoor recreation in Alaska. Wool retains 60% of its insulating properties when wet, and most synthetics do better than that. For adamant cotton enthusiasts, light cotton garments can be worn under wool or synthetics for comfort, then removed if sweat accumulation makes them cold on the skin—which is common in cool weather. The new synthetics (like Thermax and Coolmax) are almost as soft as cotton and a lot more comfortable–even after just the slightest sweat buildup in a cotton garment. Visitors often go on day trips with only the clothing on their back, so they should make it a policy to dress in clothing that is the most efficient at keeping them warm—and alive—under any possible circumstances. Personally, I wear less cotton as the activity becomes more remote or more likely to encounter mishaps.

Since staying dry is such a high priority, hikers and campers also need to have an established procedure for water crossings to avoid mishaps. Always unbuckle your pack (even day packs) when crossing moving water. (While crossing in a boat, these items should be off your back.) Packs should be dropped if you slip while crossing fast-moving water where your life might be at stake. Before crossing, you should determine how dangerous the water is and make a plan if you do slip. If there is a danger of being swept downstream, tie a short length of rope on your pack with your walking stick tied to the other end and plan on releasing them if necessary. After you are safely across, it will be much easier to retrieve your pack and the stick with a rope between them to snag on rocks or logs. If the stream is narrow but fast, you can also tie your pack and walking stick together with a rope that goes loosely around a log on the beginning side; and be prepared to drop both if necessary. If you complete your crossing without mishap, just untie one end and pull that free end around the log and back to you.

Hikers should also have a policy about crossing ice. Follow the water-crossing precautions about unbuckling your packs as well as releasing them—think ahead so you are not caught unaware. It is always best to go around ice whenever possible, but if you must cross, carry a stout pole at least ten feet long. A strong pole will likely support you if you fall through and then help you get out of a hole and back onto solid ice by yourself.

Clothing Selection Guidelines 85

Hooded jackets are very important when trying to stay warm. A hood can retain over 50% of the body heat we lose in cool or cold conditions—as when viewing a glacier from close up.

In addition to water crossings, there are other reasons you might get separated from your pack and gear. Anytime you are traveling in remote areas by plane, boat, horse, or even off-road land vehicle, always remember that accidents do occur. Plan for your survival; you might have to depend on what is on your person. Therefore, another good policy is to always carry survival items on your body. Matches (waterproof or in a waterproof carrier), a knife, map, and a compass—in order of importance—are good items to habitually carry on you when involved in any phase of a backcountry trip. These items will help get you out of most unexpected situations in good health. For better insurance if staying out overnight is a real possibility—a pocket-size space blanket, a few firestarters, disposable hand or bodywarmers, and some trail food can also be carried in large pockets.

CLOTHING CHARACTERISTICS

Important factors to consider when selecting your clothing for an Alaskan adventure are weight, bulk, cost and durability. Many Alaskan trips require off-road travel by horse, plane, boat, ATV or with a backpack. Clothing which is lightweight and compact is always preferable in these cases, particularly on backpacking trips where every ounce is carried on the hiker's back. Those who make it a habit to consider weight and bulk will have a more functional wardrobe, useful for a wider range of traveling conditions wherever they go.

Cost is also a factor for most people. By selecting clothing with a wide range of uses, you can maximize productivity of your traveling budget. Durable clothing will help cost-conscious travelers reduce replacement costs, as well as prevent possible field disasters. Travelers should be able to rely on their clothing (and equipment) to carry them through demanding situations encountered in Alaska or other destinations. Clothing should be tough enough to last for the duration of many years of traveling trips to the mountains of Alaska or the desert canyons of Colorado, where enjoyment as well as personal safety are dependent on tough, functional clothing.

FABRICS

The most definitive aspect of clothing is its fabric. Every material used for outdoor garments (and other gear) has distinctive characteristics. It is necessary to understand these traits to make the best choices of clothing.

Fabrics can be evaluated by their insulating value, toughness, comfort on the skin, breathability, wind resistance, and moisture resistance, absorption and retention. All these factors affect how a fabric will function in the field and should be considered when selecting clothing.

Natural fabrics include cotton, silk and wool. A common characteristic of these natural fibers is their tendency to absorb and hold moisture. This tendency is their biggest downfall for most Alaskan situations. Clothing which holds moisture next to the skin will cause a significant amount of heat loss by evaporation. Unless you are in very hot weather conditions–unusual in Alaska, you need to be warmed and not cooled by your clothing.

Cotton is the most popular clothing fabric because of its comfort next to the skin, quietness, durability and low cost. Cotton's biggest drawback for most Alaskan situations is its tendency to attract and hold large amounts of moisture. Wet cotton has little or no insulating value. It is very cold when wet and dries slowly. This is the main reason cotton should only be used in hot weather when the temperature does not drop below 60° F, when dry clothing is readily available, or when you can get indoors when you do get

Cotton clothing is great for warm summer days at the beach.

cold. But having to go indoors because you are cold will detract from your experience.

In hot weather, cotton can help cool us by trapping moisture and holding it next to our skin. In cool or cold weather, this tendency to hold moisture can put us at high risk of hypothermia or at least make us uncomfortable. This is why many people (myself included) in northern climates wear cotton clothing sparingly on outdoor adventures, certainly not on camping trips or even day hikes into remote areas. (For exclusively indoor purposes, however, cotton is my favorite fabric.) There are news stories every year about people who venture short distances into Alaska's wilderness and fall victim to hypothermia because they are wearing cotton clothing. After a rain or a minor accident which results in their clothing getting wet, they are unable to get warm and their body temperature slowly declines and hypothermia sets in. Cotton is comfortable and I wear it often, but not on any Alaskan adventures which could become life-threatening.

Silk also absorbs and holds moisture, but not as much as cotton. Silk feels great next to the skin and some people really enjoy wearing it. This is fine as long as you are not going to rely on it to

Wool clothing is a good choice for outdoor clothing in Alaska.

keep you warm. Silk is only semi-durable, has little insulating value and is costly. Treat silk as you would cotton. It is comfortable and that is its only redeeming quality for Alaskan wear. It is fine for wearing within cruise ships' indoor areas, for dining in city restaurants or under a weatherproof layer for a daytime walk on Alaskan city streets.

    Wool clothing resists moisture somewhat and has been a longtime favorite of outdoor enthusiasts. However, it does absorb a lot of moisture when exposed to several hours of rain or heavy perspiration and then is extremely hard to dry out. In cold weather, when dry clothes are available, or when external heat sources are available to dry clothing each night, wool clothing can be a good choice. However, I don't recommend it for fall backpacking trips in Alaska. I did wear wool pants on my overnight camping trips in Alaska twenty years ago, but discontinued that after one rainy trip when my pants got soaked on the first day. For the duration of that backpacking trip, my pants were wet and extremely cold. It still chills me just thinking about it; I ended the trip early because of it. Wool clothing is also heavy and restrictive during physical exertion–like climbing the mountains here in Alaska.

Clothing Selection Guidelines   89

Wool does have some attractive characteristics. Good wool is breathable, tough, quiet, non-reflective and somewhat warm when damp. The abrasive fibers of wool clothing irritate skin and warm the wearer, even when wet. However, this irritating characteristic makes wool unwearable for some people. This is the reason some manufacturers of wool clothing suggest wearing non-wool underwear–which defeats one of the purposes of wearing wool in the first place. Another drawback of wool is the difficulty of cleaning it without significant shrinkage and cost.

A great variety of surplus military wool pants are also available at much lower cost than the expensive woolens often offered in catalogs; and I have found these low-cost pants to sometimes outperform those expensive name brands. Several brands of wool shirts are also available which, again, can outperform the expensive models. Allowing for the drawbacks noted, wool is by far the most useful of the three natural fibers for outdoor use in Alaska.

Synthetics are the class of fabrics which justifiably makes up most outdoor clothing today. The most obvious advantage synthetics have over natural fabrics is the way they interact with water. Since our bodies produce about 20 ounces of perspiration per day, our clothing must be able to deal with this moisture and still keep us warm and comfortable. Many synthetic fabrics are engineered to attract body moisture and wick it away from the skin. Moisture which stays next to the skin will cause cooling by evaporation—a little of which is okay when you are overheated from hiking—but excessive cooling is what leads to hypothermia–the number one threat to your safety in the Alaskan outdoors.

Unlike natural fabrics which actually absorb moisture *into* their fibers, synthetic fabrics absorb moisture *between* their fibers. This allows a much larger percent of excess moisture to be wrung out or shaken out of synthetics than from natural fabrics (like after a mishap around a body of water). Additionally, the remaining moisture trapped *between* synthetic fibers dries much quicker than moisture which gets trapped *inside of* natural fibers. This is very important to hikers and campers who have to deal with rain, perspiration, and stream crossings and who depend on their clothing to make them safe and warm in Alaska's outdoors.

Synthetic clothing can be comfortable, water-resistant, warm, tough, lightweight and affordable. However, there are dozens of synthetic fabrics to choose from and not all offer the qualities necessary for good (Alaskan) outdoor clothing. Critical research and scrutiny can uncover the best fabrics for your needs.

Fleece (also referred to as pile) is one of the most popular synthetic fabrics used for outdoor garments. Fleece is made of 100% polyester, it is hypoallergenic (non-irritating), a good insulator, comfortable, repels water, absorbs very little moisture and dries quickly. It is also affordable, washable, lightweight, durable, breathable, and quiet. Its drawbacks are: it doesn't block the wind well by itself and it is bulky. There are numerous varieties of fleece. Some of the brand names are Polarfleece, Polartek, Polartuff, Polarlite, Microfleece, Arctic Fleece, and Stealth Fleece. Clothing made from any of these has its own mix of the qualities mentioned and must be examined individually by the prospective buyer.

Although the bulkiness of fleece garments is fairly similar between brands, wind resistance varies quite a bit. It is improved in some garments by the addition of a windproof layer. WindStopper® and WindBlock® are two materials with a windproof layer added. However, this does add to the weight, breathability and ability to dry quickly. For backpack camping, it is often better to wear a windproof layer outside of your fleece when necessary. Then the two layers can be separated and dried much faster. When traveling on cruise ships or any other mode of transportation that includes a warm room at night, there will be ample opportunity to dry single layer fleece garments with a windstopping layer. You can determine which garment best suits your needs.

There are many other synthetic fabrics widely accepted for outdoor clothing. Base layer fabrics (for garments worn next to the skin) include Thermax, Coolmax, Thermastat, Capilene, polypropylene and many others. Their biggest selling point is their ability to wick moisture from the body and dry quickly. This and their softness make them comfortable to wear. For most Alaskan situations, synthetic underwear is a far better choice than cotton or wool. Remember, staying dry in Alaska is an imperative for staying comfortable and safe.

Clothing Selection Guidelines   91

Water-resistant clothing—like these synthetic jackets and pants worn by hikers on the Chilkoot Trail—will keep you much more comfortable when many sources of moisture are all around you.

Synthetic fabrics for an insulating or protective layer include brand names like Worsterlon, Supplex, Microtex, 3SP and generic fabrics like nylon, polyester and acrylic. Again, their main selling point for clothes is their water repellency. The one drawback to many of these fabrics is they are noisy. This can spoil the outdoor experience for some people because they cannot hear nature plus it is disconcerting to hear only the loud swishing of your clothes as you walk through a crowded room. Worsterlon is one that is not noisy, as well as being comfortable, durable and affordable. I use it exclusively for my outdoor and traveling shirts, however I dislike Worsterlon pants because they drag too much when I am climbing. 3SP is a fabric made by Sporthill which is excellent for serious hiking or cross-country skiing pants. I use a pair on many of my outdoor excursions here in Alaska. They are warm, tough, wind-resistant, very water repellent, fast-drying, lightweight, compact and comfortable–everything I look for in outdoor apparel. As more synthetic fabrics are being developed almost daily, experience by yourself or someone you know is the best way to discover which of the newest synthetic fabrics might suit your needs. Personal experimentation is costly and time-consuming so, whenever possible, what I do and what I suggest is to solicit opinions from other people who have used different fabrics.

For an insulated outer layer on really cold trips north (or anywhere the temperature may drop to 0° F or lower) the choices are down or synthetic insulators. Down has a great warmth-to-weight ratio and is used extensively in cold climates. In below-freezing weather, down is a good choice. I have a pair of down pants that I've worn on subzero snowmobile rides down to -85° F, and never even felt the cold. They are great when there is no chance of rain. However, in the future when I have to buy extreme cold weather gear I will opt for open-cell, polyurethane-foam, insulated gear from Northern Outfitters™. Their gear is used by many dog sled mushers in Alaska and Canada for good reason. The foam has insulating qualities similar to down, but it doesn't absorb moisture like down. During extended cold weather camping this becomes a prime consideration. When down gets wet its insulating qualities are reduced to almost zero and it is difficult to dry.

Synthetic insulators like Thinsulate, Hollowfill, Qualofill, Primaloft, Lite Loft, Polarguard and the open-cell polyurethane foam are better choices in cool, damp weather, and sometimes even in cold weather because of their water-resistance. Some of the newer insulators like Lite Loft and Thinsulate are able to compete with down's warmth-to-weight ratio and down's compactibility (unfortunately some are also comparably priced). Outer layers of synthetic-filled garments are a safer choice when the temperature may hover around the freezing point and produce rain instead of snow. A hiker or camper with down clothing must be very careful not to get soaked in this situation or he may face a real threat from hypothermia (which can lead to death from exposure). Backpackers with synthetic clothing may have to carry a few more ounces of clothing, but will be in considerably less danger of hypothermia.

WATERPROOF FABRICS

The outermost layer of clothing suitable for many Alaskan days should be water-resistant or waterproof. There are many (supposedly) waterproof fabrics to choose from and more are being offered each year. The only absolutely *waterproof* fabric is rubber. Good rubber rain wear will stop all water from coming in from the

Clothing Selection Guidelines 93

exterior, but it also stops any moisture from getting out from the interior. Since our bodies produce moisture constantly, this means after a few hours of standing or sitting we will begin to feel damp from the inside. Just twenty or so minutes of vigorous exercise will also dampen the inside of rubber rain wear. Rubber is also heavy and bulky. Rubber rain wear is not very practical for most situations. The one exception is when fishing or sight-seeing from a small boat where keeping out lots of water is often necessary and weight is not a concern. Otherwise, most visitors need to look to the next best alternative to rubber to stop moisture intrusion into their "street" clothes.

The ideal rain-wear fabric for any situation would stop water from getting in from the outside and also let body moisture pass through to the outside. Anything less and you will not stay completely dry. This ideal is the target of the growing number of waterproof-yet-breathable fabrics. GoreTex is the best known of this type of fabric, (in reality GoreTex is a membrane intended to be laminated between two fabrics) and it does an okay job of keeping water from coming in but letting body moisture go out. Other brands of this type of fabric (or membrane) are Cool Dri, Dry-Plus, and Omni-Tech. Although a hard downpour or prolonged rain will drive some moisture through even the best of these fabrics, they do keep most of the moisture out and the wearer comfortable.

This polyurethane-coated nylon raincoat is lightweight, compact, and will keep this fisherman dry for hours in a hard Alaskan rain–good insurance for an enjoyable experience.

The quality of seam-sealing when making the garment, how clean it is and its age all greatly affect the performance of these fabrics. All of these fabrics tend to be fairly quiet (by rain wear standards), slightly bulky and costly. Even so, I highly recommend that any visitor to Alaska have at least one outer garment made of one of these materials. They are very versatile and can keep you comfortable in a wide variety of the weather conditions Alaska has to offer.

Layering is a commonly used practice for winter sports. It should also be used during the other seasons to control your temperature, perspiration and overall comfort. These factors are much easier to control by adding or removing several thin layers, rather than one or two thick garments.

Other fabrics good for rain wear include polyvinylchloride (PVC) laminates, polyurethane-coated (PU) nylon, and waxed cotton. Waxed cotton is almost waterproof but also heavy, expensive, and needs periodic refinishing to keep performing. Both PVC and PU fabrics are fairly waterproof, fairly quiet, compact, lightweight, inexpensive and tough. I have been using various PU suits for over twenty years for backpacking, camping, fishing, and hunting here in Alaska. I have also had GoreTex rain suits and have been satisfied with them—except for the price. As the price on these garments has come down and I am more able to afford them, I now buy more GoreTex (or similar fabric) garments because they keep me more comfortable for a wide variety of uses—like traveling.

Regardless of the type of fabric used, there are some features which are necessary for a good rain suit. As with most clothing, large pockets with Velcro-closed storm flaps are always handy. Thigh-length coats are usually preferable to waist-length rain coats, both so they can be worn alone and with hip boots and still keep us dry. The coat should also have a hood with a drawstring and a stiff, projecting bill to keep driving rain off our faces and glasses. The coat should be cut full to allow for layers of clothing underneath.

Clothing Selection Guidelines

There should be adjustable Velcro closures at the wrists and all seams should be factory-sealed. The main zipper should have a protective storm flap with Velcro closures.

Rain pants should have a drawstring plus elastic at the waist. Any slash pockets to provide access to inner pants should have a storm flap with Velcro closures. Pant legs should be full enough to admit boots without removing them; zippers on the lower legs with storm flaps are preferable.

LAYERING

One basic principle to dressing properly for outdoor activities is layering. This concept refers to using many layers of thin clothing instead of one thicker layer. This approach to dressing makes the best use of different fabric types by using each where they are most effective; i.e. as a base, insulating or protective layer. Layering also allows you to add or remove clothing during the day to remain warm without excessive perspiration.

A base layer consists of briefs, t-shirt and long underwear when necessary. Base layer clothing should be comfortable (soft) against the skin and have the ability to wick moisture away from the skin. Synthetics are ideal for base layer clothing as they wick moisture well and do not hold moisture like cotton will. I remember on one of my many camping trips to the Alaska Peninsula I felt unusually cold the first day. That night, I realized why I had been cold when I discovered my cotton "traveling" shorts were still on– they had held perspiration against my skin and cooled me unlike my "camping" Thermax briefs–which dry quickly.

The second or insulating layer does just what the name implies, it insulates. The thickness or number of insulating layer(s) depends on the level and variations in temperature expected. Insulating layers may consist of shirts, pants, bibs, vests, sweaters and coats in moderate temperatures. In cold weather, more or thicker layers of any of these and/or an extra layer or two of fleece long underwear may be called for. Except in very cold weather, it is better to add two thin layers rather than one thick layer to permit more temperature control. This is particularly important for a hiker or camper who expects to climb for several hours and then sit on an exposed hillside and enjoy the view for another few hours. During any rigorous exercise, it is best to remove as many layers as necessary to control perspiration. Remaining just a little cool during physical exertion will prevent moisture buildup and keep clothing as dry as possible for any "standing" part of the trip. A hiker or camper with dry clothes will be warmer, more comfortable and in much less danger of hypothermia.

A protective layer should stop wind and rain–always possibilities in Alaska. It may be just a heavy shirt, light jacket or raincoat. In more extreme weather conditions it may be a heavy, wool mackinaw; an insulated, synthetic, waterproof parka; or a thick, down parka with a hood. The number and variety of layers necessary depends on the possible weather conditions and variations in levels of activity. When I go fishing on a boat where I don't do much physical exercise and I will sit for most of the day, I sometimes wear just a few thick layers. When I am going hiking or skiing in cool or cold weather I usually have five, six or even seven thin layers which I can add or remove as necessary–depending on my level of activity and the temperature.

Gloves and mittens are another part of the protective layer. There is an endless array of these in all designs and materials and no one variety will suit all conditions here in Alaska. When wet weather is possible it is best to use wool or synthetics, as cotton or leather will quickly get soaked and be almost useless. I find that wool keeps me warmer than synthetics in wet weather. In cold weather when moisture isn't a prime concern, I switch to a synthetic shell (usually nylon) with a thick liner or down mittens. Gloves or mittens with built-in windproof layers are also warm, but also take longer to dry. Those with removable liners make drying much easier. I have a box full of a variety of types and pick and choose depending on the conditions I expect. The best strategy for remote trips is (whenever possible) to take more than one pair to cover different conditions and always have a dry pair. I suggest all visitors bring a pair of light wool or synthetic gloves just as a precaution, regardless of the season. They don't take up much space, are inexpensive, and will suffice in most situations the average visitor will encounter. Those visitors who are coming to watch Alaska's Iditarod in winter or planning on hiking extensively will, of course, have additional gear for their hands.

Clothing Selection Guidelines 97

A hood and a wind-resistant jacket should be available anytime you are on the water in Alaska–even sunny summer days.

The final and most important part of a protective layer is a covering for the head. A bare head may dissipate up to 50% of the body's heat production at 40 degrees Fahrenheit and up to 70% at 5 degrees. It is critical to your warmth and safety to always have good head gear available. Any trip in Alaska at any time of year might be cool enough that a hat will be needed for you to be comfortable. A good hat should cover the ears and neck when necessary and be windproof for optimal warmth. Watch-cap type hats are better than no hat, but a better style hat for colder conditions is a facemask type or balaclava which covers all of the head and neck when needed. The best varieties of balaclavas now have a windstopper layer included which doubles their effectiveness. Another good hat style is the billed cap with long, fold-down ear flaps that fasten under the chin. These cover most of the head and neck, come in water-resistant synthetics and have a waterproof/windproof layer inside. This is a good hat style for the casual summer visitor who is not going on any remote trips. A simple baseball style hat is okay for mild weather to keep off the sun and a little rain, but it shouldn't be depended on for much warmth. Hat styles with continuous brims (cowboy or river guide styles) are also useful to protect us from bright sun or rain in mild weather, and they do provide a little warmth.

Hats are a crucial element in the protective layer of clothing. This man's smile conveys his enjoyment of the Alaskan experience, which is directly affected by his comfort level. He looks warm and dry.

For most hat styles, synthetic fabrics are a good choice because of their water resistance and comfort. Wool is okay for warmth, but it soaks up water and is uncomfortable for most people. Down hats and hoods are good for cold weather visits when moisture is not a concern. For the warmest hats in cold weather fur is the best. Properly constructed fur hats are absolutely windproof and the first choice of people living in the coldest regions of the earth. The fur also traps warm air around the exposed face and keeps it warm without covering it. My personal beaver hat is so warm that I can only wear it when the temperature is below zero degrees Fahrenheit, but there is nothing to compare to this hat when it gets really cold. Visitors who plan to spend time outdoors in the extreme cold weather of an Alaskan winter should consider a fur hat.

One concept for hikers, campers, or cold-weather (spring or fall) fishermen to remember when dressing for cold weather is that the human body's first priority is to keep its core temperature at the proper level. Extremities—like hands and feet—are a secondary priority. When the core temperature begins to decrease even slightly, the blood supply to hands and feet is restricted to keep all possible warmth for the core. This mechanism can result in cold extremities if we under-dress, no matter how warm our mittens or boots are. To prevent cold hands and feet, make sure to dress sufficiently from your legs to your head to keep the body core warm. On the other hand, when our core temperature gets too high, more blood is pumped to our hands and feet to cool us. So the first thing to do

Clothing Selection Guidelines 99

when you get overheated is to remove gloves and/or mittens. If you are still too hot, removing your hat will disperse excess body heat very quickly. This cooling/heating mechanism of our body became really apparent to me on one of my winter trips here in Alaska. I was on Nunivak Island off the western coastline of Alaska in February–the coldest month of the year. My body was dressed so warmly that when there was no wind my hands would stay warm without mittens or gloves at 30 below zero. My body was pumping so much blood through my hands to cool itself that they stayed warm, though exposed, at this extreme temperature. This mechanism is the reason for the old saying, "If your feet (or hands) are cold, put another coat on."

CLOTHING SELECTION

The ability to match garments to the season, weather and type of adventure you are planning is important to having comfortable trips–wherever you may go. Some of the factors which should be considered before each trip are:

1) Can several changes of clothing be taken, or is weight and bulk a limitation? –as when backpacking or flying to camp when it is necessary to take the lightest combination of clothing which will keep you warm and dry in all possible weather conditions.

2) Will there be a heat source to dry gear out at night or is it a cold camp where moisture will build up over the course of the trip?

3) Will you be moving most of the time, stationary or some mix of the two? How much clothing is needed and how thick should the layers be?

4) How much clothing can you afford or are you willing to buy for a trip? Will a few clothes have to suffice for many types of traveling destinations?

Some other strategies to remember when choosing traveling clothing are:

1) Buy clothing large enough to wear layers underneath when needed without restricting movement, and buy it ahead of time to allow for a trial run to test it before the actual trip.

2) Be willing to make alterations to clothing to suit you. The addition of large billows pockets or pant leg zippers are common alterations I make.

3) Suspenders free up your waistline for added comfort and less perspiration during activity or when other layers have to be added, but make sure and buy synthetic models and not cotton which will retain perspiration and feel clammy until you can dry them.

Weather can be unpredictable. These two skiers stopped for a 30-minute sun break when conditions were perfect for beach attire. Thirty minutes later, after the wind came up, they had to don complete winter clothing to stay warm.

4) Dark clothing attracts more biting insects than light-colored garments.

5) When tent camping, extra clothing can be put into plastic (Zip-Loc or vacuum-packed) bags within duffel bags to keep them completely dry.

6) An emergency rain poncho can be made out of a large plastic bag with holes cut for the head and arms. It is even a good idea during heavy downpours to put one of these over your (almost waterproof) raincoat or pack to keep out all moisture.

7) Suggestions of traveling friends, acquaintances, local inhabitants, tour operators and lodging personnel can be invaluable when looking for new garments or traveling into different conditions or regions.

Clothing should keep you warm, dry, comfortable and safe. An understanding of available fabrics and designs is helpful—as is personal experience—to discover what works for an individual in each type of weather condition. Learning how to select the wardrobe which best enhances your trip will greatly improve your traveling experiences.

CHAPTER FOUR

FOOTWEAR EVALUATION

Proper footwear is one of the most important items in your Alaskan wardrobe. Visitors often walk long distances or spend long hours on their feet and must have warm, dry footwear if they expect to get the most of their experiences. Warmth, comfort, style, safety, effectiveness, durability and moisture resistance are all qualities to look for in the proper Alaskan footwear.

SELECTION OF FOOTWEAR

The type of trip you are planning is the first thing to consider when selecting boots or shoes for an Alaskan visit. Comfort is arguably the top priority for visitors who depend on their feet to carry them through the many possible adventures in "The Great Land." Besides just plain fitting well, warmth and moisture resistance are the other important factors determining the comfort of footwear. Durability, cost and safety are additional factors to consider when selecting gear for your feet.

As with clothing, the material footwear is made of determines how it will function in the field. Leather has long been the favorite material for boots and shoes because of its strength, durability, support, moisture resistance and protection it provides. With the addition of relatively new waterproof linings (like GoreTex), leather shoes and boots are still the best in many outdoor situations. In warm weather conditions, canvas shoes are often used because of their light weight and greater ability to dissipate moisture and heat. However, don't bring them to Alaska unless you plan on using them exclusively for indoor activities. I've seen many visitors with soaked and chilled feet after even a light rain. Alaskan temperatures will make you suffer anytime you get your feet wet.

Rubber and other waterproof materials (vinyl, plastic) are other options for footwear. The ability to keep moisture out should be the primary concern when choosing these materials for footwear. Their biggest drawback is retention of moisture around the feet, which will probably lead to chilled feet and perhaps detract from a day's adventure. The best way to overcome this is to plan a way to dry these types of footwear regularly and/or change socks frequently—even during the day.

Boots with liners made of materials like felt and Thinsulate are a good option when cold weather is expected. Boots with liners are often much warmer and are made for a wide variety of temperature ranges. Liners which are removable allow you to always have a dry pair to wear on alternating days. Footwear which is simply insulated can be good in cold weather, but is hard to dry if too much moisture builds up. Careful inspection of the boot's components will be necessary to discover if this may be a problem. As before, synthetic insulation will be easier to dry than natural materials like wool. My personal hiking boots have Thinsulate insulation, a Cambrelle lining (both of which dry incredibly fast) and a GoreTex layer to keep out moisture. This combination has kept my feet warm and dry many times in below-freezing weather combined with heavy perspiration during long climbs.

One more factor to check out when choosing footwear is their weight. Heavy boots or even shoes will noticeably slow down anyone who has to walk or climb any distance. The old mountain man's guide is that one pound on your foot is the same as five pounds on your back. I witnessed a firsthand demonstration of this claim while hiking several years ago in the Talkeetna Mountains of Alaska. After losing one boot during a river crossing I had to finish the three-day backpacking trip wearing a pair of tennis shoes. I was amazed at how fast and effortlessly I was able to climb a 2,000-foot slope with the lightweight shoes on compared to my usual heavy foot-

Footwear Evaluation

Today's footwear can keep your feet dry and warm, yet be durable, lightweight and good looking. These New Balance® 962 Country Walkers with GoreTex are a great all-round shoe for traveling in comfort and style.

wear. I practically ran up the hill with a full pack. If anything, I would say the one to five ratio is an underestimation of how heavy boots can slow you down.

Once a material is chosen the construction of the footwear should be the next consideration. Quality construction is of utmost importance for demanding hiking situations to protect feet. Even for walking city streets, quality footwear is important for comfort and protection. Inadequate or low quality footwear is the leading cause of sore, blistered feet, or just cold feet and negatively affects the experiences of Alaskan visitors and residents alike. Footwear must be constructed not only to endure tough Alaskan conditions, but also to fit an individual's foot. The only way to ensure this latter requirement is to go through a rigorous fitting process every time footwear is chosen.

THE RIGHT FIT

It is always best to try on shoes and boots before buying. I will only buy them from a catalog if I have previous experience with the identical model of shoe or boot. At the least, make sure any footwear you purchase through a catalog are returnable for a full refund or exchange. Feet are each unique (right to left, as well as person to person) in their design, shoe and boot manufacturers use different lasts and sizing charts, and feet change with age. All of these variables and more make footwear selection a difficult and necessarily personal endeavor. Anyone who expects to consistently select properly fitted footwear without investing some time and effort is unrealistic.

First, try both feet when fitting any footwear. Almost everyone has one foot which is larger than the other, so using only one foot will not tell you if *the pair* fits. Second, wear the same socks and the same insoles as you will wear in actual conditions–for obvious reasons. This means you should buy leather boots (which have a bothersome habit of stretching and shrinking) one-half to one full size larger than city shoes. It is easy to add another liner or another pair of socks to boots which are slightly too large after stretching, but perfectly fitting boots which shrink are hard to deal with in field conditions. Try every angle of step and put pressure in all directions in the fitting room to ensure you get a good fit. You will thank yourself for your diligence after every mile you travel with your new footwear.

BREAK-IN PROCESS

Many types of footwear available today need little breaking-in to be ready for use, but it still helps to mold them to your feet under controlled conditions. Leather boots particularly will shape themselves to the wearer's foot when wet. Even old leather boots can be reshaped somewhat. The tried-and-true method of doing this is to get the boots soaking wet and then walk them dry. As the leather dries it molds itself to the foot it surrounds. Of course this may take many hours and miles, but it is worth it if you are about to embark on a once-in-a-lifetime trip to Alaska or another destination you've dreamed of all your life. Even if the trip just entails being on board a cruise ship for seven days with a few stops in Southeast Alaska, your footwear is important to the outcome. Certainly your feet will thank you and you will have a more enjoyable trip if you go through a proper break-in process for your footwear.

Footwear made of canvas, synthetics or other materials should also be tested before any traveling. Adjustments like adding or removing the appropriate insoles, wearing two pair of thin socks instead of one thicker pair, or just lacing in a different manner should be tried before leaving home. I have a pair of mountain boots with plastic shells and insulated liners which can be difficult to walk in, but I have discovered that by lacing only the bottom six pair of

Footwear Evaluation 105

These Danner® Sierra Hunting Boots are lined with Thinsulate™ for warmth and GoreTex to keep out water. They also have deep lug Vibram® soles which grip well in most terrain. I've owned a pair for years and they are great boots.

eyelets I can walk much more comfortably on flat ground. This little adjustment has saved me a lot of time and discomfort over many years of mountain hiking. Now I am very attentive to any new footwear to see just how comfortable I can make them by testing variations in socks, liners, insoles, and lacing patterns. Your feet are too important to ignore any possibilities that would improve comfort.

WATERPROOFING

Manufacturers' recommendations should be followed about what to apply and how to apply it when waterproofing new footwear. After paying up to several hundred dollars for top-of-the-line shoes or boots it is only sensible to spend a couple dollars for the proper water sealant. Boots (and some shoes) which are properly treated will keep your feet drier, conform better to your feet (which means fewer blisters) and last longer. Leather footwear should be warmed slowly to no more than 100° F before applying a waterproofing substance. Placing footwear in direct sunshine for a few hours or in a furnace room are both good ways to warm them. A quicker but riskier method is to place them in a *warm* oven. It is best to leave the oven door open to reduce the chance of cooking a good pair of boots.

Once the boots are warm, apply several liberal layers of the chosen waterproofing substance, letting each layer soak into the leather between applications. The more thoroughly the boots have been warmed and the thicker the applications (1/16th to 1/8th inch) the more waterproof the boots will be. Just thinking back to times when you've had wet feet should prompt you to do the most thorough job possible. The first few applications to new boots or to boots after a long, wet hike will be completely drawn into the leather, leaving a dry surface. Applications should be continued until the last one remains on the surface. This can then be wiped off with a clean cloth leaving the leather completely saturated with the sealant.

Materials like canvas or nylon often require spray-on silicon for water protection. This usually requires cleaning and drying the surface before several applications are applied, with drying periods in between. Again, warm footwear will accept more of the sealant and result in a better waterproofing process. These silicon-based sprays can seem expensive, but not when compared to how much money is invested in the footwear and the overall trip. A few dollars for dry feet is a small price to pay when it means so much to the enjoyment and success of a trip.

FIELD CARE OF FOOTWEAR

The objective of finding appropriate footwear and properly caring for it is comfortable feet. And the most important requirement for comfortable feet is to keep them dry. After proper selection and care of shoes or boots before a trip, the next requirement is to keep them as dry as possible in the field. The first thing to

Footwear can make or break some visits to Alaska. Snowmachining, dog mushing or watching the Iditarod are two examples.

Footwear Evaluation

remember is to take any opportunity to dry footwear in the sun. If you are hiking and stop to sit and take a rest during a long climb, removing your boots to take advantage of a warm sun can greatly reduce the moisture buildup during the course of a long trip. Placing shoes and boots in the warmest possible place at night is also a good habit. This usually means a high place in a cabin or tent or near the heating source in a room.

When tent camping, an evening fire can be used judiciously to help dry boots. Be careful about getting leather boots too close to the high heat of a fire as it can damage them. A safer way to use the fire is to first heat small rocks, then place them inside a sock which is then placed inside the boots overnight.

One very effective way to dry boots is to use small, disposable handwarmers available in most northern states. These inexpensive devices last anywhere from five to eighteen hours and produce a safe level of heat to dry any footwear. I discovered this application after years of camping on the Alaskan Peninsula and wearing wet rubber boots for weeks. Now I place one of the small, inexpensive handwarmers into each of my rubber boots at night. In the morning 90% of the moisture buildup will be gone and I often have warm boots as a bonus. During the three weeks I annually spend in an unheated tent on this trip, this little trick makes for a much more comfortable experience.

One more thing to consider about leather boots is resoling them. If you have a good pair which are really comfortable, but the soles round off so they are not as effective on steep slopes or slippery trails you can consider this option. As long as the leather uppers are still in good shape a new sole can be attached to extend their useful life. Plastic mountaineering boots can also be resoled by a good cobbler.

SOCKS

Socks are almost as important as footwear. They are often a major factor in your comfort level. Good socks help keep your feet warm, dry, and blister-free.

A sock's material defines many of its qualities. Cotton socks can be comfortable in warm climates or indoors, but because cotton

ThorLo's are the best socks ever made—bar none. They cushion and massage your feet, resist moisture, dry quickly, are very durable and look good. I wear them about 350 days per year.

holds moisture and mats after just a little use, they are not good for most outdoor activities in Alaska. Wool socks provide a lot of warmth and are a favorite for cold weather activities. Even after a full day of hiking and sweating, wool socks keep some of their loft to warm and cushion feet. However, wool blended with synthetics retains more of its loft, is warmer, and quicker to dry. I prefer 100% synthetic socks because they retain most of their loft to cushion and warm feet even after long days of backpacking. They are more durable than wool or cotton, less abrasive than wool and dry quickly. The best socks available (for any purpose) is a brand called ThorLo™. They have a patented weave design which massages the foot and feels very good all day long. They also have cushioning pads under the heel and ball of the feet without any annoying edges where the cushioning begins. They come in dozens of varieties for any sport or purpose imaginable. They are made of a blend of mostly high-bulk Orlon with minor amounts of wool or other synthetics. They retain an incredible amount of loft even after days of brutal, sweaty backpacking, hold very little moisture and dry quickly even in unheated tents. They are so good to my feet that I wear these socks almost exclusively 365 days a year. They cost at least $6 a pair, but they out-last any other sock as well as feel very good. They are worth the extra cost. There are numerous other brands of synthetic socks which are good, but, for my money, none are quite as good as ThorLo™.

In extremely wet conditions hikers can also use GoreTex socks. These socks will keep feet dry for at least several hours even when footwear is soaked on the inside. Under adverse conditions it is very comforting to know you can put on cold, wet boots and have dry feet. Although some moisture will eventually seep through these membrane-type socks in extreme conditions, they may be worth carrying for the most physically demanding hikes. Before these socks were available, I remember one mountain backpacking trip when my leather boots were soaked and frozen solid each morning. I had to endure one to two hours of excruciating cold each morning until the boots thawed and then warmed up. Having a pair of these socks would have kept my feet dry at least until the boots thawed out and were warm, and made for a much more enjoyable trip.

AN EFFECTIVE SOCK STRATEGY

Developing an effective *sock strategy* is necessary for maximum foot comfort. For traveling in warm climates a thin sock of almost any material may suffice. For Alaska's colder weather, one thicker sock or multiple layers of wool or synthetic socks are called for–the thickness and number of layers being determined by the temperature. People whose feet sweat excessively may consider carrying an extra pair if they plan on walking a lot so they can change into dry socks when the first pair gets damp. Thick socks are often better for standing or sitting still as on the deck of cruise ships where little walking is done, but two or more layers of thinner socks is better when considerable walking may be required. Wearing two pairs of thin socks will help prevent blisters better than one thick sock because the inner sock will grab the foot tightly and not rub against it as one thick pair of socks often does. Using a layering approach also allows another pair to be added during the day as the boots loosen, as they heat up or as they get damp from sweating or outside moisture. Once feet start to move around inside boots sore spots can develop at rubbing points. A quick stop to add or change a sock layer can prevent rubbing and avoid blistering.

Even when heavy wool socks are preferred, a synthetic liner sock is usually best for inside the wool layer. Thin liners of polypropylene, Capilene™ or Thermax™ are smooth and aren't as abrasive to feet as wool can be. Synthetic liners also have less friction against an outer sock layer so they can move independently–precisely what they should do for maximum comfort. Silk liners will serve the same purpose, but they retain more moisture and don't dry as quickly as synthetics.

FOOT MEDICINE

Even the best socks and layering techniques will not prevent sore feet under the most demanding hiking conditions. The foot owner's next layer of defense is foot powder, Toughskin™ and/or Moleskin™. Applying foot powder before donning socks helps reduce friction and hot spots which can become blisters. Toughskin™ is one brand of liquid coating which creates a "second skin" over hot spots or blisters to prevent further damage. Moleskin™ is one brand of self-adhesive padding which can be placed over potential or actual blisters to protect them. I have used Moleskin™ over open blisters and backpacked for several days with no further aggravation of these sores. It is amazing stuff, and I never travel without it.

The last—and I believe most important—strategy for every foot owner to know concerning feet is elevation to reduce swelling. Gravity causes fluid to build up in our feet–particularly after a long day of walking or hiking with the extra weight of a backpack. The fluid buildup results in swelling of our feet which usually leads to soreness and blisters. The best way to avoid this is to elevate your feet for 15-30 minutes at night. Pregnant women are told to do this same thing to drain excess fluids and reduce swelling caused by the extra weight their feet are supporting. People who suffer from swelling feet or ankles from other reasons like arthritis can also benefit from this practice. Bar none, this is the best solution I have found to caring for my feet during my weeks of backpacking I enjoy every year here in Alaska. For anyone with sore feet from any kind of walking or standing, I highly recommend this simple, yet effective method to reduce swelling and discomfort.

In most traveling situations, you depend on your feet to carry you through a successful vacation. There are very few traveling experiences which will not be adversely affected by poor footwear or cold, wet, sore feet. Therefore, learning to buy the proper foot gear and how to care for your feet properly is an important step to becoming a successful traveler.

CHAPTER FIVE

PHOTOGRAPHY, CAMERAS & BINOCULARS

"A good snapshot stops a moment from running away."
                                                    -Eudora Welty

Photographic reminders of our past travels are what keep the memories alive in our minds to enjoy for the rest of our lives. When we begin to forget the details that made a vacation memorable, photos can bring back all the sights, moods, feelings and companionship that made it a great experience.

SUBJECTS TO PHOTOGRAPH

Those who routinely take a good variety of quality photos will maximize their enjoyment of their traveling (and life) experiences. The scenery, weather patterns, companions, etc. are all part of a trip and should be recorded on film. The best strategy is to take numerous photos of a variety of subjects. After the trip is over, photos can be sifted through and just the best ones retained for a photo library of memories.

The subjects you choose to photograph on a trip vary with each experience, but the following list is a good starting point.

MODES OF TRANSPORTATION – cruise ships, airplanes, railroads, automobiles, taxis, off-road vehicles, small boats, pack animals, walking, hiking, climbing, etc.

ROOM/LODGING – arriving, sleeping quarters, lodge vistas, lodge setting, lodge personnel, mealtime, etc.

WILDLIFE – animals, birds, marine life, pets, etc.

TOUR PERSONNEL – boat captains, tour directors, bus drivers, taxi drivers, outfitters, locals, etc.

SCENIC SHOTS – from planes or boats, local history, sunrise, sunset, weather extremes, terrain extremes, etc.

TRAVELING COMPANIONS IN ACTION – any activity

MOOD SHOTS- weary travelers, relaxing in evening; –remember to take unposed shots to get the sincere mood of the traveling experience.

After learning *what* to photograph, *all* travelers need to know *how* to take good photos. Everyone should be able to take photos of others so memorable photos of all traveling companions are taken.

COMPOSITION

One key to taking good photos is thinking about what the final photo will look like. Think about professional photos and what makes them pleasing to the eye. You must consider positioning, viewpoint, shape, color, scale and focus. There are some guidelines for good photography, but no absolute rules. Variety and experimentation will often produce some great shots that break one or more of the guidelines of good photography.

Positioning and viewpoint are the two ingredients of composition in good photography. The guideline for positioning is called the "rule of thirds" (see Diagram 5.1). If a photo is divided into thirds with four imaginary lines (the dotted lines), the four points where these lines intersect (the small circles) show the best locations to position the subject. Positioning a subject or the horizon in the center of a photo typically produces a dull picture; the exception is when the subject has strong geometric lines and is symmetrical–like a rectangular building. You should apply this "rule of thirds" to most photos. Experimenting with different positions in the frame will usually indicate where the best position is for a given subject and view.

Viewpoint refers to where the photographer is located when taking the photo. One good guideline is to get close when there is one main subject–like a shot of a person's mood. Filling the frame with the subject provides emphasis to photos. When photos are taken from a distance the subject can be lost in the background,

Photography, Cameras & Binoculars

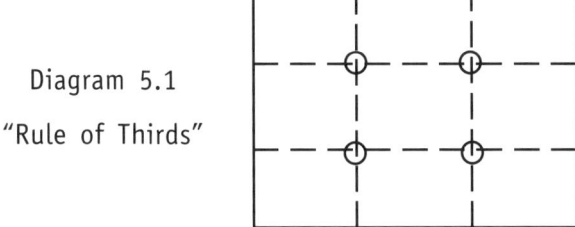

Diagram 5.1
"Rule of Thirds"

resulting in a dull photo. However, when the background is important to the composition of the photo, the photographer must back up a sufficient distance to properly frame all of the subject.

Trying all angles and distances will improve the variety and quality of your photos. Lie down, stand on top of something, get real close or step back and look through the viewfinder. This kind of experimentation with viewpoint can help any photographer improve his/her photo composition.

Viewpoint also changes the shape and relative size of your subject(s). One common technique is for the photographer to get very close to a person and position another subject several feet behind them. This helps emphasize the main subject (the person) while still making the secondary subject an important part of the photo. This is a useful technique to remember when a photographer wants to emphasize any subject in the foreground, not just people shots.

Lighting is another critical part of taking quality photos. There are several guidelines to remember. Don't take photos directly into sunlight or artificial light–unless you are backlighting or silhouetting for emphasis and you adjust the exposure setting accordingly. On overcast days remove as much sky as possible from the photo to avoid underexposure of your subject. Use a flash or fill-flash in low light conditions. Have people remove or adjust hats to avoid shadowed faces, or use a fill-flash if you are within the flash's range. Move around the subject as you look through the viewfinder to discover where the light best shows off your subject. Often just changing your position or having your subject move a few feet will make the difference between a discard and a great photo. Sometimes if you wait for clouds, fog, rain showers, or snow squalls to move in or out, they can provide better lighting, a dramatic background or affect the mood of the photo.

Learning the photography skills needed to capture wildlife like these Dall porpoises on film does take time, and getting the right equipment and film is an important first step.

Additional guidelines for top quality photos include holding the camera as *still as possible* and *gently* squeezing the shutter to get sharp pictures. Only hand-hold a camera when using a short lens at fast shutter speeds; shots at less than 1/30th of a second need to be taken from a tripod or other stable platform. Use shutter speeds of at least 1/250th when shooting from moving vehicles. Use a high aperture setting for maximum depth of field when taking scenery photos. Don't position your subject too close to the edges of the frame. This often results in part of it being cut out or so close to the edge that it distracts the viewer. Make a habit of using the center outlined area for both focusing and light meter adjustments and then adjust the framing of the subject. With auto-focusing cameras the typical procedure for this is to 1) hold the shutter release halfway down while the light meter makes the adjustments, 2) keep the release partially depressed while you frame your photo, 3) and then fully release the shutter.

One key to good photography is to take *lots* of shots. After all the time, effort and money that is spent on a once in a lifetime trip, it is a shame not to spend a few minutes per day and a few rolls of film to record the memories for future enjoyment. As an Alaskan who has entertained many visitors, I have taken many rolls of film of Alaskan experiences. I have never had a visitor complain about too many photos, and have gotten many heartfelt thanks after the photos came back.

One important thing to do in anticipation of a photo is to remove unwanted objects from the background. Carefully examining the scene through the viewfinder before taking photos will identify these distractions so they can be removed or the angle changed to exclude them. If a tree or another object in the background of a

Photography, Cameras & Binoculars

photo would appear to be growing out of someone's head, change the angle or have the person move slightly. If extra clothing or gear is scattered in the background and detracts from the photo, move it. Don't let scenery or background subjects detract from or ruin a photo. Look through the viewfinder with a critical eye when composing and the main subjects of your photos won't be compromised. Good photography takes a little planning and attention to detail.

Don't forget that cameras malfunction and film processors make mistakes. For insurance against these and other hazards always use parts of two rolls of film (finish one roll and start the next) when important subjects are being photographed and even use two different cameras when possible. A disposable camera can be used for the extra camera in case of malfunction, and they actually take pretty good pictures. A few dollars spent ahead of time may save a lost photo opportunity of a lifetime. And make sure to carry extra batteries for your main camera. Give yourself every opportunity to get great photos of a trip. Few visitors make an Alaskan trip for less than $1,000, and for most it is many times this figure. I can't imagine not taking every precaution to get good photos, since this is a once-in-a-lifetime trip for many of these people. With this level of investment, a few additional dollars for an extra camera is certainly justified.

TRAVELING CAMERAS AND FILM

The camera you choose to take on your Alaskan trip can have a significant impact on the quantity and quality of your photos. For most purposes a small point-and-shoot 35mm is a fine choice. A traveling camera should be light and compact enough so it will always be available and not left back in your room or packed away somewhere. As the name implies, the point-and-shoot models do almost everything for the photographer. A full-size 35mm camera is capable of more and takes better photos in some conditions than the point-and-shoot models, but they are much bulkier, more expensive and require more expertise.

In addition to the auto-features commonly found on most point-and-shoot 35mm models, there are a few features which the optimal Alaskan camera (for nonprofessionals) should have. A waterproof model is essential for traveling in wet weather and is good insurance in case of accidental submersions in even the driest climates. Here in Alaska I have lost three cameras to moisture buildup which eventually led to malfunctions–usually during a trip. My current camera is waterproof to 10 feet underwater, and it has lasted much longer than the previous, non-waterproof models. However, I still carry my camera in a Zip-Loc to protect it from moisture, dirt and physical abuse.

A timer is also essential on a traveling camera to take pictures of everyone in the group. Other features like zoom lenses, an auto shutoff and a panoramic mode may improve your photos, but they are not really essentials. If you do want panoramic photos of Alaska's great scenery, you can buy a disposable camera with this ability. Just remember they are very expensive to develop.

Once you buy a camera, the first thing to do is *read the manual*. This not only helps you avoid simple blunders, but you will know the capabilities of your camera, probably learn something about photography in general and take the best photos possible.

There are a few simple guidelines when choosing film for Alaskan photography. Color slides or black and white prints are best if you plan to sell them. Otherwise, most people choose color prints for personal use. However, one thing to consider is the current advances in home photo printing. My computer scanner has a slide/negative adapter which lets me make color prints directly from these sources. There are also stand-alone units for home use made for photo printing. In the past, it cost several dollars each to have prints made from slides at a photo shop. Not any more. I can make color prints from slides for less than 50 cents each. The advantages of taking slides are the color is much better, the developing is cheaper, they store easier and they maintain their color longer.

Any brand of photo film will suffice. The quality of the developing can significantly affect the quality of your photos, so if you have some one-of-a-kind photos on a roll of film, choose your developer carefully. The more expensive photo shops will usually do a much better developing job than you will get from a photo booth in your local variety store.

The film speed you should use depends on the amount of light available when the photos are taken. ASA100 is used for daytime shooting in bright light situations. ASA200 is used for conditions

Photography, Cameras & Binoculars 117

Compact 35mm cameras are great for most people who are not experienced enough with full-sized cameras to use them well. A waterproof, compact 35mm, like the Olympus at left, is a good choice for an Alaskan visit and it can take very good photos with just a little practice.

with less than bright light, like overcast days. ASA400 is used for low-light levels–like at dusk. Anything outside of this 100-400ASA range is generally used by professionals who know the specific applications. ASA200 is a good all-around film to have with you to cover most situations. I carry mostly 200ASA as my standard film and some 400ASA for lower light photos, or if I will be exposing an entire roll using a flash. Whatever film you choose, take twice what you think you will need. Film will keep until the next trip and it is cheap in relation to the price of most vacations. Don't run out of film and "let the moment run away."

BINOCULARS

Although the initial outlay of cash is daunting, purchasing high-quality binoculars is a good investment into improving your traveling experiences. Good binoculars will last for ten, twenty or even thirty years with a little care. Even a five-hundred dollar set of binoculars amortized over twenty years is only twenty-five dollars per year. That is a small cost to significantly improve your enjoyment of twenty years of traveling.

Like cameras, binoculars for an Alaskan visit should be waterproof. I always recommend bringing only waterproof optics to Alaska. I have discarded my share of binoculars and cameras over the years which weren't waterproof and learned the hard way. Alaskan weather can be wet almost anytime of the year, and in many locations, you can count on wet weather during any two-week visit. Binoculars which aren't waterproof will often fog up overnight if they are put away just a little wet. And the changes in pressure due to elevation changes, so common to Alaskan travel, will force moisture inside even the most expensive binoculars in a few hours if they aren't waterproof.

There are some characteristics to look for when shopping for any type of optic (binoculars included). Look through the optic to check for clarity of the image. The quality of the lens helps determine this as does the anti-reflective coatings on them. The best optics are multi-coated on every lens surface to reduce reflections and improve light transmission. Single-coated lenses should be avoided by those who want the most from their optics–regardless of cost. A thorough in-store comparison of optics will show you which ones are brighter and clearer. Brightness is important for those who want to see in low light conditions. Brightness is also affected by the size of the objective lens, which is the one farthest away from the viewer. The trade-off for larger lenses is increased bulk, weight and cost.

The size of binoculars you buy depends on the intended use. Magnification of seven to ten power and objective lenses of from 25 to 50mm are the ranges for most brands. If you will only buy one pair, 8 X 42mm's are a good all-around choice. In binocular descriptions, the first number indicates the magnification and the second number is the size of the objective lenses. For most uses, 8 X 42's aren't too large to carry all day, but have enough magnification and brightness to be used for hours of glassing without eye strain. Binos with over ten-power magnification can be hard to hold still enough to get a clear view. Several hours of looking in this manner will tire out the user's eyes and diminish his or her ability to see clearly. Binoculars with objective lenses above 50mm may bring in more light, but they can be bulky. Size does not necessarily mean more brightness, so don't buy on this criterion alone. Quality is always the most important thing to consider.

Compact binoculars may be the most useful for most travelers. Sizes of 8 X 25mm or 10 X 30mm are common compact sizes. Ten-power compacts may have too much magnification for some

Photography, Cameras & Binoculars

All binoculars for Alaskan use should be waterproof. These Cabela's full-size and compacts are waterproof, armored and relatively inexpensive.

users, but others like them. Brightness is often reduced in the compacts, but good glasses will still gather a lot of light and brighten the view. Compacts' biggest selling feature is their small size and weight–often less than 10 ounces and small enough to fit in a shirt pocket. As with compact 35mm cameras, because of their small size and ease of carrying, compact binoculars will more likely be available when you need them.

All binoculars should have a center focus ring. It is quicker and just as reliable as individually focusing rings on each barrel. A strong, wide carrying strap is mandatory for binos which are often carried for hours every day. Rubber armored binos are a little heavier, but warmer on the hands and more durable for those willing to carry the extra weight. Binos should also have eyecups for keeping your eyes the correct distance from the lenses and to reduce glare in bright sunshine. I'll never forget one bespectacled visitor I met who didn't know what these were for. He complained that during his twenty-odd years of binocular ownership he never had much use for binoculars because the aperture was so tiny. He had never pushed in the eyecups, so his eyeglasses kept his eyes too far away from the lenses to see well. When I pushed them in for him, he was flabbergasted at how well he could see.

Cleaning optics correctly can preserve their usefulness for a full twenty or more years. Any dust or grit will scratch a lens surface if it is rubbed. To avoid scratching lens coatings or even the glass itself and damaging your optics, treat them as carefully as an expensive camera. The first step is to blow off dust with an air brush like those used for cameras or by lightly blowing on the lens. The next thing to do in optimal conditions is to flood the lens with distilled water, roll it around a little, pour it off and air dry. If this doesn't remove all the smudges, use lens tissue with a small drop of lens cleaning fluid on it. Rub gently in a circular motion with as little pressure as possible to clean the lens. One option for field cleaning is to carry a lens-cleaning pen made specifically for hunters to clean their optics. Since these pens place a solid surface on the lens, be as gentle with these as possible to avoid damage.

If you have nothing else when you need to clean a lens, a soft, clean tissue or soft, clean piece of fabric will do. First blow on the lens to remove dust or water. Then gently brush the lens surface with the clean material using as little pressure as possible. This is the most common way lenses are scratched, so keep this practice to a minimum. Proper cleaning products and gentle handling will keep your optics in top condition and provide you with bright, clear images for many years.

Photos like this one are priceless. Taking lots of good photos takes a little time and some forethought, but the results are well worth it.

CHAPTER SIX

LUGGAGE STRATEGY FOR ALASKA

Alaskans are unique in many ways, even in the ways we carry our clothing and gear. One factor which has influenced the size, shape and construction of our luggage is the available transportation here in "The Great Land."

Maybe one-tenth of Alaska is accessible by road, and that is only accurate if you include all the back trails which are usable only part of the year by ATVs. Much of the travel we do here in Alaska is by small plane or boat. Both of these modes of travel often place restrictions on the size, weight, number and construction of parcels they will carry. Sometimes these restrictions are absolute, and sometimes they will be expanded for exorbitant fees. The result is that we (Alaskans) have learned the easiest, safest and least expensive ways to transport our gear within Alaska.

HARD-SIDED LUGGAGE

Hard-sided luggage is the old standard for air travel. This is still an acceptable option for air travel into the major cities of Alaska, for air travel within Alaska on smaller commuter airlines, for some cruise ships headed for Alaskan ports and for automobile travel to Alaska. Disadvantages of hard-sided luggage are the extra weight, limited space inside, rigidity (takes up more space) and odd shapes. The newer soft-sided luggage which has a fixed shape (as opposed to duffel bags) is sometimes a better choice for cruise ships and for travel within Alaska–both on small planes and small boats. The advantages of soft-sided luggage are reduced size and weight for the same amount of contents. It also tends to be more rectangular so it packs into small planes and boats more efficiently. If you do choose to bring this type of luggage, select quality brands because Alaskan transportation methods are tough on luggage.

Many Alaskans have opted for duffel bags to transport gear within Alaska when space and weight are at a premium. These flexible parcels fit into small airplanes, small boats, railroad cars, buses or on ATV's better than hard-sided luggage. Some of these bags even come with shoulder straps and/or wheels for transporting short distances when necessary. It is best to select a duffel bag with more space than you expect to need–there always seems to be one more thing to put in it. However, be aware that most airlines—including those in Alaska—have a 100 inch and 70 lb. limit for baggage. The 100 inch limit is the total of the length, width and height. This restriction is not always enforced and soft duffels seem to get by more than either hard or soft-sided luggage, but some attendants may enforce this if your bag is too cumbersome. The 70 lb. limit is almost always enforced nowadays, so be careful about packing your luggage. A good strategy is to be prepared to remove a few items and put them in your carry-on if you are over the size or weight restriction. Duffel bags are also a good choice for backpackers who place their packs inside. They can often get by with one bag with a pack plus other gear inside which still weighs less than the 70 lb. limit. For charter planes or boats within Alaska, which don't count number of bags but are concerned with weight, the pack can be taken out to make two smaller pieces which are easier to pack in a small plane or boat.

Features to look for in duffel bags are strong two-way zippers, large rip-proof straps sewn all the way around the bag for toughness and a method of fastening both straps together. When both straps are fastened together it prevents baggage handlers from grabbing one strap at a time which is more likely to cause damage. Waterproof material, double or triple-stitching and wide straps for packing are other desirable features. Water bags made for canoeing and kayaking are a good choice for Alaska if you are going to be traveling around water or sleeping in a tent. Many Alaskan "Airports" do not have quick baggage service and your bags may be precipitated upon, so waterproofness is a desirable quality for all

Luggage Strategy 123

Traveling Alaska's waterways in luxury boats like the Discovery (see copyright page) is one of those unforgettable life experiences. However, most water craft in Alaska have space limitations on the luggage you can bring. Soft-sided, water-resistant luggage is the best choice for this type of voyage.

your luggage. These waterbags come in all sizes and shapes just like duffel bags and will even float when properly sealed. It is a good practice to use plastic bags within all bags which travel in Alaska to ensure dry gear. Even "waterproof" duffel bags and waterbags leak at times. It is a simple, cheap way to guarantee dry gear in even the wettest conditions.

Small commuter airlines and air charter services within Alaska are the most common transportation services who will put tight restrictions on your luggage allowance. If you check with each service you intend to use and plan accordingly, you can save headaches and some extra fees you haven't budgeted for. Carrying an extra duffel bag inside your luggage is one way to be prepared to alter your luggage as needed.

Another consideration is the U.S. mail service in Alaska. Mail service within Alaska is subsidized by the government, making it one of the cheapest methods of transporting heavy packages within

Alaska. On return trips if you have acquired extra "stuff," it is often possible to mail heavy items you won't need immediately and save hundreds of dollars in extra charges from the air service. Even mailing items home from Alaska is an option if you gathered stuff (clothing, gifts, souvenirs, fish?) which will cost you dearly to carry home. We Alaskans often carry perishables (fish or game meat) as luggage and ship home clothes we won't need for weeks, thus saving on exorbitant charges for luggage.

Individual tour operators—whether they are cruise ships, bus tours, railroad tours, etc.—will usually have recommendations or absolute restrictions on the luggage you can bring along. Listen to their advice because they usually give out good information and their restrictions will often have to be observed. Plan your luggage so you can meet all the restrictions on the various transportation services you use while keeping cost to a minimum. There is no need for your Alaskan trip to be more expensive than necessary.

CHAPTER SEVEN

GEARING UP FOR ALASKAN CAMPING

The most important consideration when choosing camping gear is to *choose the right fit*. Backpacks, tents, sleeping bags and other gear must not only fit the person, this gear must also fit their style of camping, personal expectations, and their destination(s) in Alaska. A tent which is unsuitable for the weather conditions is as much a liability to a camper as an ill-fitted backpack or inadequate sleeping bag.

The first sources of information a camper should consult are friends and acquaintances who have used similar gear. They can often start the camper on the right path to gear which fits his or her specific needs. Better yet is trying out the gear you are planning to purchase either from a friend's gear cache or a rental room from a local sporting goods store. The minimal option to getting a good fit between camper, camping style, Alaskan destination and gear is careful hands-on inspection or analysis of the product's description before purchasing. Competent salespeople can often help, but don't rely too heavily on their opinions if you have doubts about their knowledge or sincerity.

A more reliable source for gear information is comparison guides in magazines like <u>Backpacker</u> or catalog comparisons (which may be biased, but at least give relative specifications). One warning when using any gear guide or catalog specifications chart–be skeptical about listed weights. Manufacturers know consumers are weight-conscious and often fudge in favor of lighter weights. Carrying a scale to stores when comparison shopping is one (extreme) way to get actual weights, but catalog shopping always has the inherent risk of dissatisfaction with product weights when they arrive. The more a camper can do to determine the actual specifications and quality of gear by paying careful attention to salespeople, catalog descriptions, and personal advice, the more likely he will be pleased with his gear's qualities and its performance.

TOUGH FABRICS FOR GEAR

There are several materials commonly used for tents and backpacks which campers should be familiar with to make good gear selections. Canvas is heavy cotton fabric commonly used to make wall tents or tepees. When canvas gets wet it swells and closes the small gaps between the threads. As long as the canvas remains taut and nothing touches it, water moves downward along the fabric without dripping through. However, if anything touches the fabric, water will be drawn through it at that point. If the object is touching the inside of a tent while it is raining for example, water will flow through the fabric onto the object and then begin to drip into the tent. Objects which typically cause a canvas tent to leak in this manner include tent frames and inner guy ropes as well as sleeping bags or personal gear. Coated canvas fabric is a little more forgiving, but will still leak in this way during any lengthy rain. Uncoated canvas can be treated with silicon or other commercially prepared sealants to improve its moisture resistance, but it will never be completely waterproof.

Canvas is also relatively heavy and hot during warm weather. Because of these drawbacks as a tent fabric, canvas has been replaced for most uses by synthetics. However, for cold weather camping when weight is not a problem, canvas is still popular. Because of its thickness it holds heat well and provides some insulation when internal heaters (gas or wood) are used. It is also relatively inexpensive and durable when properly dried and stored.

Cordura nylon is a heavyweight, stiff, abrasive-resistant, rough-textured, wind-resistant, durable fabric used for packs, footwear, duffel bags and protective gear cases. Plain cordura repels moisture fairly well, and coated cordura is virtually waterproof. Packs and duffel bags made of cordura should be checked for a water-

Alaskan Camping

Alaska's rugged mountains are undeniably beautiful, but also dangerous. If you are planning a camping trip in Alaska's remote areas, be sure your gear is tough enough to withstand the terrain and the weather.

proof coating; this makes these items much more serviceable for travelers and campers.

Ripstop nylon is a lightweight, supple, synthetic material with larger threads every 1/4 inch or so—giving it a characteristic checkerboard appearance—which stop small rips from becoming gaping holes. It is used for coat shells, outerwear, stuff bags and lightweight gear coverings. Ripstop is not abrasion, wind or water-repellent by itself, but can be made fairly wind and waterproof with the proper coating. To check for a waterproof coating on any synthetic fabric, look for a shiny side (usually just one side is coated) produced by the coating. This shiny side should always be on the inside of gear bags or garments to reduce abrasive damage to the coating. Polyurethane is the most common substance used for waterproofing synthetics. Rain gear and packs using this coating agent will list it on their labels for conscientious buyers who read labels.

Nylon taffeta is a soft, supple, lightweight synthetic used for linings in clothing. It is not abrasion-resistant or water-resistant.

Polyester taffeta is similar to nylon taffeta, but more water and UV-resistant, so colors don't fade as much as they do in nylon taffeta. Both taffetas are often coated for water resistance.

Almost all synthetic materials can be made more water-resistant by applying spray-on silicon. This commonly comes in aerosol cans available specifically for this purpose where sporting goods are sold. Following instructions on the spray can and any cautions on the gear will enhance the results.

Fasteners come in a variety of forms, each with different characteristics. For outdoor use, nylon zippers are usually much better than metal because they are warmer, quieter and less affected by water and cold temperatures. Two-way zippers are useful on duffel bags, long raincoats, and protective cases. Coil zippers are preferable where strength and durability are important.

Buttons are reliable fasteners, but they do come off at inopportune times and are slow. Velcro is much faster for pockets which are frequently opened, rain covers over zippers, sleeve closures on raincoats, and draft hoods on sleeping bags. Experienced campers often alter gear to suit their needs, and adding or changing fasteners are easy ways to change many types of gear to better serve your needs.

TENTS

Tents come in an ever-increasing array of sizes, styles and grades. There are three-season, four-season, single-wall, double-wall, triple-wall, freestanding, dome, tunnel, cabin-style, tepee-style, A-frame, floor-less, bivy sacs, modular tents and more. Anyone who plans to use a tent in Alaska should have at least a general understanding of the characteristics and purposes of each tent style to make the proper selection(s).

The purposes of a tent are to provide warmth and protect its occupants from sun, precipitation, wind and insects. These qualities along with durability, ease of erection, comfort, size, weight and cost are what to look for when tent shopping. Catalogs often offer charts which allow for quick comparisons between the tents they sell. This is the best place to start looking for a new tent. However, remember to treat weights and non-measurable descriptions with a little skepticism. Tents described as "three-person" are often a good fit for two. It is better to rely on the square footage of floor space for size comparisons, but even this has to be balanced against the steepness of the tent wall of each design to see how much *usable* floor space there actually is. As with all gear purchases, use common sense and try to imagine every possible good and bad feature before you buy.

Design is a primary consideration. Moisture intrusion and removal are important factors affected by design. Remember that an average person gives off a quart of moisture during eight hours of sleeping. Any additional time or activity in the tent will also increase the amount of moisture inside. Optimally, all this moisture should be passed to the outside of the tent.

Design and construction are both features to consider when choosing a tent to keep you dry and safe in Alaska's (often) wet weather.

Keeping precipitation and dew out of a tent and allowing inside moisture to escape is best accomplished in one of two ways. The most common construction strategy to achieve this is a two-layer tent; the inner tent is not waterproof, the outer layer is waterproof and there is an air space between the two layers. Precipitation falling on the outer layer simply runs along this waterproof layer down to the ground. Moisture inside the tent can pass through the permeable inner layer to the air space–where air circulates and removes the moist air. The better double-wall tent designs with an outer, waterproof fly also have a waterproof floor which extends 6-12 inches up each side wall of the inner tent layer. This keeps any minor collection of ground water from coming in through the walls. Also, since the waterproof fly should not quite touch the ground to allow good air circulation to remove moist air, this "bathtub style" design stops any errant precipitation which may pass under the fly and reach the inner tent walls from coming into the tent.

The alternate construction strategy is using a single layer of one of the semipermeable fabrics like GoreTex. Small molecules of water inside the tent are theoretically passed to the outside, but larger water drops are not supposed to penetrate the pores of the fabric into the tent. The advantage of this tent design is (hopefully) lighter weight since there is only one layer of fabric. However, their moisture transfer performance is not as good as two-layer tents, and they generally cost more. Canvas is another example of single-layer tent construction whose qualities have already been discussed.

Large tents with vertical or near-vertical walls and high roofs make comfortable base camps in areas with wind protection or mild weather. These large tents can be heated with properly vented gas stoves or wood stoves with a stove jack through the roof. Single-layer canvas is commonly used for this type of tent. It is relatively inexpensive and durable if properly dried and stored between uses. Single, double, or triple-layer nylon tents are also available in this design–the multilayered models providing more insulation for colder weather conditions. Nylon tents also come in geodesic or dome shapes which provide almost as much room as wall tents, but are often lighter, less bulky, more wind and water-resistant, and easier to erect.

Another possibility for a main camp tent is a tepee. Single-layer tepees shed wind and water well because of their steep walls and rounded shape. Their steep wall design also provides lots of head room compared to floor space, and they are the ultimate design for having an open wood fire inside a tent. The fire's smoke flows directly out the top hole around the poles. Its one major drawback is bulk. The long poles needed for construction are difficult to transport as is the large amount of tepee material.

The shape and construction of a tent will determine how well it withstands wind and rain. Generally speaking, tents with lower, more streamlined profiles will shed both wind and rain better. Most four-season tents have rounded or very slowly sloping shapes, low peak heights, more poles and are made of heavier material than three-season tents to withstand the rigors of winter weather. Their drawback is the extra weight, bulk and cost. Three-season tents intended for milder weather often have more sharp angles, vertical sides, higher peak heights and are made of lighter materials. This provides more floor space per pound of weight–which is a critical

Alaskan Camping 131

Even after choosing quality, appropriate gear for an Alaskan visit, it still pays to act prudently. Here I have placed my tent under an overhanging rock for additional weather protection.

factor when backpacking. Because they often have lighter material and more bug screening in place of heavier fabric, three-season tents usually allow air and moisture to pass out of the tent better than four-season models. The result of all these differences is that three-season tents are preferable when four-season strength is not necessary. Experienced backpackers using three-season tents will allow for their lack of strength by placing these tents in more protected areas.

Most tent poles are made of fiberglass or aluminum. Fiberglass poles are heavier and less costly than aluminum poles. Hollow fiberglass poles are lighter than solid fiberglass poles, but also break easier. Good aluminum poles are stronger than either types of glass poles. Some tent manufacturers offer both options for their tents and sell replacements. Backpackers usually opt for aluminum poles because of the weight advantage. Also, aluminum poles which are bent in the field can usually be straightened and/or reinforced sufficiently to be serviceable through the end of a trip–at which time replacements can be purchased. Broken fiberglass poles, however, are much harder to repair satisfactorily in the field. A very few tents can be poled with local small trees—like some wall tent styles and tepees—but this is not practical for most situations.

Bivy sacks are small, single-person bivouac tents. They sometimes incorporate one or two hoops to hold tent fabric off the occupant, but others are just large, un-insulated bags which are designed to lay on top of the occupant's sleeping bag or just directly on a clothing-clad backpacker. Most incorporate some brand of "waterproof-yet-breathable" material to reduce weight and are more accurately described as water-resistant. They also don't breathe very well so a considerable amount of moisture collects on the inside.

The primary advantage of using one of these bivy sacks is their light weight and small size–often under two pounds and sometimes under sixteen ounces. These personal shelters are practical in mild weather and for short periods, but few backpackers are tough enough to use these uncomfortable "tents" for other than an occasional, "Rambo-style" hike. Their advantage is questionable since standard-construction, one-person tents under two and one-half pounds and two-person tents under four pounds can be found which provide much more protection and comfort for just a couple more pounds; and the camper(s) will be drier, more rested, and more likely to enjoy the experience.

A more practical, single-person shelter for weight-conscious backpackers is a small, waterproof tarp with several grommets. If there are physical features like large boulders, cliffs, deadfalls or brush in the area, a tarp can be quickly fastened into a comfortable shelter with a little cord or rope. Finding a suitable location to do this takes a little experience, more time each evening (compared to a tent) and the result may not be as roomy or convenient as a tent. Plus, when there is severe weather or a large number of insect pests, a tarp may not be a good choice. However, you can purchase a good six foot by six foot tarp for under $20 which weighs under a pound and use it comfortably in more situations than most backpackers believe possible. I have been much more comfortable during the nights I spent under a small tarp than the times I have used a small bivy sack–and the sack cost ten times as much!

There are a few other tent pointers to keep in mind when shopping for or using tents. Having a small area (called a vestibule) outside the main tent, but inside the waterproof fly makes a conve-

The vestibule on the entrance to this tent is convenient for storing wet gear, for cooking (with the door <u>open</u>), and to help keep moisture out of the tent.

nient place to store wet gear or cook in inclement weather. The trade-off for this convenience is more weight and higher cost, so balance your priorities and choose accordingly. Also, remember that any tent (or vestibule) must be adequately ventilated to operate a stove inside safely. Many people have died from using even small stoves inside a closed tent which rapidly lowers oxygen below safe levels. Tents are also very flammable, so use caution with any fire source which can quickly destroy your only shelter and any gear stored in it, perhaps leaving you suddenly with few clothes and gear in harsh weather– a survival situation.

On warm nights or during rainy weather, tents with *good* circulation are much more comfortable. Better circulation is often accomplished with more insect netting panels in the inner tent fabric. Some tents are designed so these panels are exposed only by opening zipper-operated fabric panels. Others just use insect netting to make up the roof of the inner tent with no fabric panels to cover them. The latter make for lighter weight tents and are common in three-season models.

Freestanding tents are supported by their poles alone. This convenience makes them easy to move once erected for exact positioning. Tents which are not freestanding require fastened guy ropes to hold them erect and are more time-consuming to move. The trade-off is extra weight associated with the poles of freestanding tents and often, extra cost.

Lastly, look carefully at construction and modify if necessary. Seams should all be double-stitched. Rain flys should provide complete coverage of the inner tent. The lower edges of flys should not be too high off the ground if the tent will be used in windy areas. Examine stakes to be sure they are the proper type for the camping area and there are enough–plus a couple extra in case of damage. Seal all seams before the first use and repeat whenever seams show any signs of leaking. Tent manufacturers or local tailors are often willing to make modifications as well as repairs (zippers?) to any brand of tent for a reasonable price. Carry a little repair tape (duct tape is good for this purpose and many other tasks) in case of field emergencies. Nylon tent flys and floors can also be coated with Thompsons Waterseal™ to extend their life and effectiveness.

SLEEPING BAGS, PADS AND COTS

The second most important piece of gear for a camper (after a tent) is a sleeping bag. No matter how cold and wet a backpacker gets, if he (or she) has a warm, dry sleeping bag to crawl into at night he can continue hiking indefinitely. Choosing the right bag is another critical decision for a successful backpacking or camping experience in Alaska (or anywhere, for that matter).

The two major factors to consider when choosing a sleeping bag are bag shape and the type of fill material. Rectangular bags are roomy, but heavy and bulky for packing. If comfort is a priority and weight is not, this bag shape is okay. Mummy bags are contoured in the shape of the human body to be as warm as possible with minimal weight and bulk. For these reasons, this type of bag is invariably used by backpacking campers. The top opening in a mummy bag should have a drawstring closure which reduces it to just a small hole for breathing, and gives it the appearance of its namesake. Another variation is a semi-rectangular bag with roominess and bulkiness qualities in between the two basic bag styles.

The type of fill used in a bag determines some of its most important qualities. Synthetic fill materials like Polarguard, Hollofill, Qualofill, Lite Loft and Primaloft repel moisture well. Even after a total submersion, synthetic bags can be wrung out and still provide most of their (dry) insulating value. The other common type of fill—goose or duck down—is useless when wet. Down readily attracts and absorbs moisture which reduces its insulating values to

Alaskan Camping

almost zero, and then is very difficult to dry. A camper who lets his down sleeping bag get wet when temperatures are below 50°F will at the least, have a very cold night, or several, until the bag dries. Under some circumstances this camper may be in serious danger from hypothermia if his bag gets wet. This is why synthetic bags are a much safer, more comfortable and more popular choice for most campers. In very cold conditions, down is still a practical choice because it has a better warmth-to-weight ratio than the best synthetics–although the newest synthetic fill materials are coming close. Down also costs considerably more than most synthetics.

Winter camping in Alaska demands good insulation under your sleeping bag. A good pad is a must if you want to enjoy—and not just endure—the experience.

The shell material for sleeping bags is almost always synthetic because of the need for a moisture-repellent fabric. Some of these materials are lighter and more abrasive-resistant than others which affects the performance of the bag. There are inexpensive bags on the market made for car or backyard camping which have cotton shells and may even be filled with a cotton mixture. Campers must be careful to avoid putting themselves in a situation where their lives depend on a bag of this type. These bags can easily become saturated and absolutely useless for providing insulation.

Manufacturers' listed bag weights and temperature ratings are some of the most unreliable gear data there is. Weight is such an important consideration for sleeping bag shoppers that manufacturers exaggerate statistics to sell their products. One thing to look at is the loft of the bag; it is one good indication of how warm the bag will be. Loft is a term for how thick the bag is–the more loft, the warmer it will keep you. There is no sure way to see through manufacturers' false claims, but personal advice and honest salespeople can be very helpful. Comparison shopping and careful study of temperature rating-versus-weight tables can also educate a shopper so unrealistic measurements may be spotted before a bad purchase is made. Simply being aware of this danger will make a consumer a little wiser and thus more likely to make a good choice.

For late spring-to-early fall mountain backpacking here in Alaska, I look for a synthetic sleeping bag which will keep me warm to at least 20° F. I have been able to find several models which do this and weigh in at about three pounds. For colder trips, you should be able to find synthetic bags which are good to 0° F and weigh about four pounds.

Features to look for in a high-quality sleeping bag are: full-length draft tubes over zippers; a box foot shape which stands up to keep toes from pressing tightly into the bag and getting cold; and a draft collar around the neck and head for additional warmth. To preserve a sleeping bag's loft and thus its temperature rating, it should be hung up or stored loosely in a large bag (fabric–not plastic) which breathes. Storing a sleeping bag in a compacted mode will reduce its loft over time, and synthetic bags are much more susceptible to this loft reduction than down. I store my bags hanging on the wall, but since I use them—and stuff them—up to 100 times a year they lose about 5° of temperature rating each year. I replace my mountain backpacking bag every two or three years and use the old one for warmer camping situations.

Being warm and dry while you are camping in Alaska is partly dependent on taking every opportunity to dry your gear.

There are also overbags and liners to improve the comfort and warmth of sleeping bags. Overbags are usually made of water-resistant material, they add warmth and they keep the bag clean. Liners are constructed of a soft material like flannel or polyester fleece which prevents cold nylon from touching the occupant's skin, makes the bag warmer and keeps the inside clean. Both overbags and liners are easy to clean compared to sleeping bags which usually have to be taken to commercial launderers or hand washed.

Sleeping pads are used to insulate a person from a cold sleeping surface–the ground or floor. The value of sleeping pads is underestimated by most people who haven't slept on a cold surface without a pad. A cold, dense surface will act as a heat sink and rob a lot of heat from a sleeping person. Conversely, a good pad will slow this heat transfer and also provide a more comfortable surface to sleep on. The best pads do this while being as light as possible.

There are open-cell, closed-cell, inflatable and self-inflating pads. Unprotected open-cell foam pads in two to six-inch thicknesses absorb moisture readily, so they are seldom used outside of permanent shelters like cabins or lodges. They are comfortable, inexpensive and less bulky than standard mattresses. Newer versions of open-cell pads incorporate waterproof barriers around the outside to keep out moisture.

Closed-cell foam pads come in many varieties. Traditional models are smooth-surfaced, dense and relatively heavy compared to newer models. Ensolite™ pads are one example of older designs. Newer designs include Ridge Rest® and Z-Rest™–two designs with surface corrugations to add comfort and insulation without adding weight. Full-length models of this type can weigh less than one pound and half-lengths can be under eight ounces for weight-conscious backpackers or campers. These pads provide more comfort and warmth than similar-size flat pads for the same weight. I buy full-length models, cut them in half and then have a second pad to use after the first half wears out.

Self-inflating pads do just that. They incorporate an inner open-cell pad surrounded by a waterproof exterior. When a valve is opened the inner pad expands and draws air inside. Closing the valve after the pad is inflated is all that is required by the user. These pads work best when they are left inflated except when transporting. Otherwise, the inner pad loses its ability to expand by itself and the user has to blow air through the valve to inflate the pad. I have one of these which is twenty or more years old and it still self-inflates because it has always been stored in an inflated condition. There are many thicknesses, lengths and widths of these pads available depending on how much weight and bulk is allowable. Single-person models can weigh up to four pounds and the half-length versions are about one pound, so these are not the best options for lightweight backpackers. However, they provide more comfort and warmth than flat or corrugated pads so are an option for shorter pack-ins or when weight is not so crucial. Another drawback to these pads is they can be punctured, so more care must be exercised with these than with closed-cell pads which are almost indestructible. The outer covering of self-inflatable pads is also water absorbent, so they should be carried in a waterproof stuff sack–which adds to their field weight.

Older-style inflatable air mattresses are heavy and provide less insulation than self-inflating designs. They are okay when transportation is available, warmth is not a major concern and care is taken to prevent punctures.

Sleeping cots can be both comfortable and a space-saving device. Extra gear can, and should, be placed under sleeping cots to free up tent or cabin floor space. Empty spaces under a sleeping cot allow air to flow freely through the void. If this air is unheated it can cool the person sleeping on the cot tremendously. Packing gear into this space will stop air flow and prevent this unnecessary cooling effect. For the same reason, pads should also be used on cots, rather than sleeping on bare cots. A sleeping person on a cot needs to be insulated from cold air or gear below the cot just like he should be insulated if sleeping directly on the cold ground. Like pads, cots also come in numerous sizes and styles. The proper choice will depend on how much space is available and how important weight is. Taller cots are more comfortable for sitting and create more space for gear storage–assuming there is enough vertical space in the shelter (tent?) to allow for them. Shorter cots with spring steel legs are usually lighter and less bulky to transport and often have rounded legs to protect tent floors. I have one of these models which has also lasted twenty years so far and is still in great shape. Sleeping cots are notorious for breaking and tipping over, so remember this when deciding how much you are willing to spend. Most inexpensive models will have to be constantly coddled to last even one trip. Generally, a few extra dollars for a better cot is well spent.

My experience with cots in tents has taught me a few valuable lessons. First, always tie sleeping pads onto cots so they don't continually slip off during the night. Simple loops of cord tied around the cot and pad will usually suffice. Second, always set up cots early and then lie in them to settle them into the ground before trying to sleep on them. Jostling around a little helps to find any irregularities on the ground surface below the tent for the cot to settle into or which may need attention. Then put extra cardboard, tent bags or duffel bags under the cot's legs to level them as well as to protect the tent floor. A few minutes of testing and leveling will be rewarded many times over by better sleeping conditions each and every night of the trip. This simple procedure is one of the habits of an experienced and successful camper.

STOVES AND COOKING GEAR

Camp stoves come in an assortment of styles, sizes and fuel requirements. Base camp stoves can be as convenient as home ranges *with* ovens–when weight and bulk are not limiting factors. These large stoves often run on large propane containers and have controls every bit as adjustable as the home variety. Base camp stoves can also be smaller one, two or three-burner Coleman-style stoves which run on bottled gas or refillable tanks of white gas (Coleman fuel) or auto gas. There are even range-top ovens for these stoves to allow baking in the field. Relying on wood stoves for cooking nowadays is questionable given the convenience of lightweight gas stoves and the limited supply of available wood in most areas (because of scarcity, wet conditions or restrictions on cutting). Wood-fire cooking also produces more smoke and soot, excess heat (sometimes a desirable by-product), requires a long

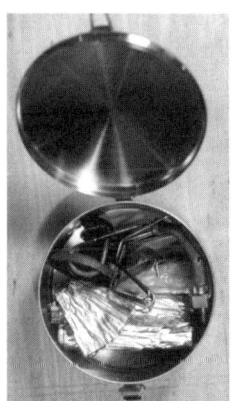

A stove/pot combination which nests together to form a compact, lightweight package is ideal for backpacking.

start-up period, is restricted at times (fire permits) and requires heavy tools to gather the fuel.

Backpacking stoves come in a great assortment depending on your needs and fuel preferences. For any type of backpacking where weight is a limiting factor, there are numerous single-burner stoves weighing under one pound for boiling water and cooking small meals. The best of these will boil a quart of water in less than five minutes and are no bigger than a large coffee cup. Mountain Safety Research (MSR) makes several models of high-quality backpacking stoves to meet a variety of requirements. One significant difference among backpacking stoves to be aware of when selecting one is their ability to be adjusted to a low heat level. Some can only run on high or almost-high heat, while the better ones can be adjusted from low to high heat for all cooking needs.

Camping stove fuels vary almost as much as the stoves themselves. Some fuel cannisters are refillable, some are not. Refillable fuel bottles can use white gas (Coleman fuel), unleaded auto gas, kerosene, or propane. White gas is the most popular fuel because of its wide availability, low cost, clean-burning qualities, efficiency and light fuel containers. The one drawback with white gas stoves is that they usually need to be primed before use. Kerosene is also cheap and plentiful, but less-efficient, smoky and stinky. However, kerosene is more available than white gas on a worldwide basis. Unleaded auto gas is slightly less efficient and clean-burning than white gas, but also inexpensive and widely available. The better models of stoves can burn all three of these fuels, although some require changing a fuel jet to burn kerosene efficiently. Propane fuel cannisters come in small to very large sizes. The five to fifty-pound variety are those used to heat backyard grills or even homes and can be used for small camp stoves. Propane is inexpensive and works well at low temperatures. Although one-pound cannisters used for camp stoves are not advertised as rcfillable, this can be accomplished with the right adapter–rather than discarding each empty container and having to buy new ones at a higher overall cost. One advantage to using propane stoves is the ability to hook them up to large containers when conditions permit carrying the extra weight and bulk. This is much cheaper and more convenient than changing small bottles, particularly when the stove is used to

Alaskan Camping   141

do the cooking for a large group of campers and/or a long time period.

Fuel types which come in nonrefillable cannisters include butane and blended propane/butane. Of these two, the blended fuel is more efficient and runs better at low temperatures. The fuel cannisters are convenient, provide good heat control and work well at high altitudes. Their drawbacks are higher expense, more weight and bulk (empty fuel cannisters to carry) and more sensitivity to low temperatures. However, newer models have improved weight/fuel ratios which rival white gas stoves.

For heating purposes, propane, kerosene or white gas models are commonly used by campers. Any of these fuels are satisfactory for this purpose as long as safety precautions are observed. These include fire prevention and proper ventilation for both exhaust and oxygen depletion reasons. For these reasons many experienced campers never leave a gas heater on while sleeping. One mistake when using gas heaters can be deadly.

Pots, pans and eating utensils are usually limited by space and weight restrictions for backpacking and for most camping adventures. The rationale is to utilize items which serve multiple purposes. Base camps often have several pots and pans of varying sizes to accommodate cooking for several people. Cast iron, aluminum and nonstick cookware are all used depending on weight restrictions and convenience desired. Camp sets often utilize nesting pots to save space. Camp cookware should be carried in a cloth pouch to avoid blackening other gear with residue soot from pot bottoms. Depending on the size and duration of the camp, cleaning items can be as simple as one nylon scouring pad or brush and a small container of dish soap. For more sophisticated camp kitchens, paper or cloth towels are handy if space permits. Eating utensils are most commonly limited to one *nonbreakable* set of a plate, bowl, cup, fork and spoon per person. Campers should have their own knives. Spares of utensils can be carried for a large camping party if space is available.

For backpacking, cookware often means one pot to boil water along with one cup and one spoon per person. This is the lightest way to go–anything above this is a luxury. Look for rounded-bottom pots for easy cleanup, tight-fitting lids and a size which will accommodate your backpacking stove to save space. Aluminum pots are lightweight, inexpensive and very popular. Steel pots are heavier and costlier, but much more durable. Titanium is very costly, but much lighter and stronger than either aluminum or steel.

Topographic maps from the USGS can be covered with clear contact paper and trimmed to make compact, durable aids for Alaskan backpacking.

MAP AND COMPASS

The more remote and unknown an area, the more important a map and compass are to a backpacker. Flat, forested areas in Alaska with no visual landmarks and watersheds which don't have obvious downhill routes are particularly easy places for backpackers to get lost. At the least, most backpackers should carry a compass, and all backpackers should have a map whenever venturing anywhere offroad in Alaska. Topographic ("Topo") maps depicting highways, roads, trails, creeks, rivers, lakes, forests, tundra, hills, mountains, ravines, etc. are useful for planning a hike as well as finding your way in new country. Topo maps are almost always a requirement for safe/successful backpacking in Alaska.

DeLorme Mapping at P.O. Box 298, Freeport, Maine 04032, (207) 865-4171, produces topographic map atlases for 27 of the 50 states, including Alaska. These map atlases contain topo maps of the entire state. It is the cheapest way to get maps of an entire state (about $20 for the atlas).

Alaskan Camping   143

The United States Geological Service (USGS) sells individual topo maps with different scales and aerial photos of much of the U.S. Their maps cover the entire state of Alaska, but they only have a few aerial photos of Alaska so far. They also have map catalogs and index maps of states for selecting which maps you want. Contact the USGS, Information Services Office, Box 25286, Denver, Colorado 80225, 1-800-USA-MAPS or (303) 202-4700.

Maps can be sprayed with a commercial map waterproofing spray or covered with a light coat of varnish to protect them for years of use. Maps can also be covered with a clear contact paper or shelving paper. This is the method I use to protect them during long backpacking trips in the inclement weather of Alaska. A layer on both sides is best for maximum protection.

At the cost of a few dollars, every backpacker should have a lightweight, compact, easy-to-use compass. When compass shopping look for a base plate with an arrow for direction of travel, a movable dial with easily readable markings, a scale index on a base plate for estimating distances and an attached mirror. The mirror is most useful as a safety device for solitary backpackers to remove small particles which may get in their eyes. Mine has saved me unnecessary discomfort or worse several times.

The first thing to do when you get a compass is to practice with it *before* going on an outing with it. At the least, this will tell you if it is working properly and teach you how its parts are supposed to function. The first thing to remember about using a compass is that it works on the earth's magnetic field, so be sure no objects are nearby which will cause a false reading. Magnets, batteries, electrical appliances, metal zippers or iron are some things which may do this.

The next thing to do is find out what the magnetic declination is for the area you will be hiking. Magnetic declination is the difference between the direction of the geographic North Pole and the direction of the magnetic North Pole. This declination varies depending where you are in the world. Since maps are made using the magnetic North Pole, you should next adjust your compass according to the declination in your current area. This is usually done by turning an outer ring on the compass the desired number of

Backpacking in Alaska's wilderness areas requires good gear. A sturdy, large-capacity, external frame pack is a good way to carry all your gear there and back.

degrees. Alaska's declination is between 30 and 40 degrees east, depending on where you are in this huge state. This means the magnetic North Pole is between 30 and 40 degrees east of the geographic North pole. Consult directions with your compass so you can use it correctly. Relying on improper usage is worse than not having it at all.

The modern alternative to a compass is a device which uses the Global Positioning System (GPS). GPS devices are now available for under $100 which are no bigger than a cell phone (another handy thing to take along when backpacking alone anywhere, and especially when out of familiar country). A GPS can tell you time, altitude, your heading, your speed, the distance from other locations, the directions back to other locations, draw you a map and tell you elapsed trip time–and probably more as new models are developed. It is a fantastic navigational tool for relocating preprogrammed waypoints anywhere on the earth, and the accuracy is within 100 feet. However, they do run on batteries which run down; so keeping a two-ounce compass on a string around your neck for a backup might be good insurance. I highly recommend a GPS for any visitor to

Alaska who intends to go off the beaten path. It is almost impossible to get lost with one of these, and it can easily save your life.

Another valuable device for solitary backpackers or even groups in remote areas is a personal Emergency Locator Transmitter. This phone-size electronic signalling device can be turned on when a backpacker suddenly faces a life-threatening injury or is trapped by weather or equipment failure. For a few hundred dollars and a pound or two it can be a cheap safeguard which can also save your life.

PACKS

A backpacker needs a proper pack. The first decision to make is whether it will be an external frame or an internal frame pack. An external frame pack has a visible frame of aluminum or nylon. Most of these can be used without the packbag as a bare frame for hauling heavy loads like firewood or large water containers. The greatest advantage of an external frame pack is its ability to haul really heavy loads. An experienced (read this to mean very strong and well-conditioned) packer can haul loads up to 150 pounds all day over rough terrain with an external frame pack. The best internal frame packs max out at 80 or 90 pounds–when they become unbearable to the same experienced packer. The difference is in the way the load is distributed. An external frame will distribute the load well between the shoulders and hips. An internal frame usually has small aluminum bars inside the pack which put most of the load on the shoulders as more weight is added–only a small percentage is placed on the hips. External frames also prevent heavy loads from shifting, whereas internal frames allow movement with each step–causing more discomfort and fatigue. External frame packs also allow the packer to walk in a more natural, upright posture, allow the load to be moved up or down on the frame and allow more air ventilation to cool the back. Internal frames also have to be loaded more carefully to prevent hard objects from poking the packer's back, whereas an external frame protects the wearer better from objects in the pack.

Internal frame packs do have desirable features for backpackers who will not have to carry more than about 75 pounds–which is the great majority of them. These packs catch less brush because of their narrower shape and they are easier to carry in airplanes and small vehicles. They are also more comfortable with lighter loads and are easier to balance because they flex with body movement– like when you are climbing through dense brush, up steep hillsides or on skis or snowshoes. This is where they have a significant advantage over external frame packs. I learned this lesson well on one long ski trip through the mountains many years ago when I wore an internal frame while my companion wore an external frame. I had a much easier ski trip, while he constantly fought to keep his balance against his stiff external frame pack. His pack made him work twice as hard on that trip as I did.

There are many advantageous features to look for in either of these two basic pack designs. The basic pack material is the first item to examine. Sturdy nylon fabric—often cordura— with a waterproof coating is the standard for most pack bags. However, very heavy material can add unnecessary weight. I buy external-frame packs, made of medium-weight nylon, which weigh about five and a half pounds and hold up well over several years of rigorous use. I don't feel the real heavy duty packs which weigh two or three more pounds and cost three times as much are worth buying. I like carrying a couple pounds less every step I take as well as buying the newest pack designs every few years. However, the heavy duty packs will last for ten years or more of heavy use and many people choose them for their durability as well as their extra features.

A pack should be the right size to fit your body. Try on several models before purchasing and ask if they come in different sizes and if they are adjustable. Packs should have padded shoulder straps, a sternum strap to keep shoulder straps from sliding too far out on your shoulders and a padded hip belt–all of which should be adjustable to fit you precisely. The pack bag should also be adjustable up and down on the frame to best balance the load on *your* back. Every person's back has a unique design.

Look for a pack with plenty of pockets in the right sizes to fit your needs. A mesh water bottle pocket is handy on the hip belt as are pockets for binoculars and a map. When shopping for a pack, remember that you can and should customize your pack to fit your individual needs. If you like dividers in the main bag then look for packs with this feature. I like one large compartment without dividers, but I have sewn on extra pockets and a climbing pole at-

Alaskan Camping 147

tachment to my pack. A little material, a few zippers and some thread and you can have a customized pack which fits your needs precisely. A professional tailor can always be found if no one in your household has the ability to do the sewing.

Look for large nylon zippers on pockets rather than small metal ones which are noisier and more likely to break. Also look for storm flaps over zippers. Plenty of tie-on points are convenient for those backpackers who always seem to have too much gear to fit into their packs. Compression straps to stop heavy loads from shifting are almost mandatory for internal frame packs.

One of the keys to enjoyable backpacking is to pack as light as possible to lighten the load you carry. This is cooking and eating gear for two–stove, pot, two cups and spoons.

Day hikers don't need a full-size pack. They can get by with a day pack or a fanny pack for the few things they will need. When shopping for one of these, look for many of the same features as on large packs. However, hikers who are not certain how large a pack they will need on their different trips might be wise to buy a modular pack. These full-size packs commonly have a detachable fanny pack, day pack and pack board which can all be used separately. This is a good way to cover all possible pack requirements when uncertain about an upcoming trip or future trips.

No matter how perfect a pack is for a particular trip, it must be loaded correctly for optimal use. Packs which are loaded top-heavy or with too much weight to the sides greatly decrease the amount of weight you can carry comfortably. The difference can be as much as 50% for the worst weight distribution. Heavy items should always be put as close to the middle of the back as possible. Food, tents and other heavy items should be put close to a packer's center of gravity. Poor arrangements cause the packer to fight the load with every step. When items have to be tied outside the pack, pick the lightest ones to put the farthest from your center of gravity.

Sleeping bags, pads and clothing are typical items which should be placed on top or tied to the back of the pack when necessary.

When backpacking, one of the keys to maximum enjoyment is to pack as light as practical and still have what you need. One way to check yourself at the conclusion of each trip is to spread out everything you carried. Except for absolute essentials like rain gear and your first aid kit, after the second time of doing this and noting an item which was not used, leave it behind the next time. This will weed out unnecessary items and lighten your load. Other ways I have lightened my load are by using only half a sleeping pad and using extra clothing as a pad under my legs and feet; repackaging food to leave behind unnecessary containers; taking only a cup and spoon for eating utensils; always considering the weight of items I might buy; and always being on the lookout for lighter gear.

MISCELLANEOUS GEAR

One mandatory item for backpackers should be a first aid kit. Hikers can get into trouble even a few hundred yards away from their vehicle, and backpackers are often days away from help. A first aid kit does not have to be complex or heavy. My kit which I take on week-long backpacks into remote parts of Alaska weighs less than seven ounces. Essentials for me are a few sterile pads, a needle, fire starters, matches, painkillers, antacids and anti-diarrhetics. Remember to include extras of any prescription medication. Each hiker's kit can be as simple or complex as needed. See Chapter Nine for more details on first aid.

A small flashlight is as essential as a first aid kit for hikers. Darkness is something we deal with every night, and it will surely come sooner or later. Having to worry about getting somewhere before dark or getting lost in it are unnecessary burdens to put on yourself. Dependable flashlights or headlights weigh only a few ounces and are very small compared to their value when needed. New batteries should be put in at the beginning of each trip and extra batteries carried in a pack or vehicle. Good models also have a spare bulb attached somewhere for the unexpected burnouts. Gas lanterns, candle lanterns and candles are other possible light sources.

Alaskan Camping 149

Putting all your gear selection, trip planning, and other camping skills together for a visit to Alaska can be very rewarding. These two lucky campers have been rewarded with a beautiful sunset on a (dry) evening in Southeast, near Wrangell.

Telescoping climbing poles are relatively new accessories which are extremely useful for mountain hiking. These are basically ski poles which collapse to about 24 inches and expand to about 60 inches. They have wrist straps, small baskets which prevent the tip from sinking too deep in tundra or poking too deeply into rock crevices and positive locking rings at the (typically) two joints. They weigh in at somewhere around ten ounces and are worth their weight in gold when descending or traversing steep hillsides–especially with a heavy load. They also let a hiker use his upper body when climbing steep inclines and provide balance on loose scree slopes. As a backcountry guide, I have had a client tell me that if I didn't provide one of these for my first-time clients, I would be irresponsible. Every client who I have introduced to these climbing poles has loved them. There were a few stubborn clients who refused to even try one to my dismay–they were slower and more at personal risk because of it. This is a vital piece of equipment for any hiker roaming open mountain slopes.

Sleeping bag selection can be crucial to the success of a camping trip. This Trans-Alaska Sleeping bag from Cabela's has down fill on top for warmth and Polarguard fill on the bottom for water-resistance. This bag is rated to -30° F, and weighs about 6 1/2 lbs.–pretty light for the warmth.

Protection from biting insects is mandatory in many areas of Alaska. On the tundra of Alaska, hordes of mosquitoes, white sox, black flies and no-seeums can actually threaten an unprotected hiker's health and sanity. Insect repellent sprays and liquids work for short periods of time, but must be applied every few hours to be effective. If several daily applications are necessary for more than a day or two the active ingredients will begin to cause skin problems. A better method of insect protection in these cases is to use head nets, gloves and/or bug jackets–garments made of bug netting which are periodically soaked in bug repellent. For camp areas bug repellent coils can be burned or devices which periodically release vaporized bug repellent can be used to make the camp area more comfortable. At a minimum, a wise traveler always carries a small bottle of bug repellent as insurance; unforeseen insect problems have ruined more than one vacation day in Alaska.

One more handy item for backpackers to own is a stitching awl. This allows a hiker to repair or modify heavy fabric or leather items he commonly owns. Stitching will often loosen or break on otherwise serviceable gear like packs, tents, gloves, etc. A few stitches is often all that is needed to stop any further damage and make the item useful for many more years. If not repaired, the item

Alaskan Camping

may jeopardize a trip or have to be replaced prematurely–an unnecessary cost if you just put in that stitch in time.

Many campers compile a gear list after many seasons to remind themselves what is needed, what is unnecessary and what is optional. Making your own gear list can save you from forgetting crucial items which requires either return trips to recover them or will cause a reduction in the enjoyment and/or success of the trip. My method of packing for a trip is to mentally go through all the possible activities on a trip and gather items as they come up in this mental rehearsal. For those who prefer a tangible gear list, the following is a fairly complete list of possible items for either camping or backpacking which can be pared down to fit individual needs. It is meant to be a master list from which other lists can be made. For example, a base camp list, a spike camp list and a backpacking list can each be made from this master list depending on which type of trip you are going on. Don't over-pack or under-pack. If you can stay warm, dry, and well-fed, you have everything you need. The right gear list will be the lightest combination that accomplishes this.

CAMPER'S/BACKPACKER'S GEAR CHECKLIST

CAMPING

__ TENT W/FLY, STAKES, & ROPES
__ GROUND CLOTH
__ TARPS
__ GROUND PAD
__ SLEEPING COT
__ SLEEPING BAG W/LINER, OUTERBAG
__ EXTRA ROPE & TWINE FOR CAMP
__ AXE, HATCHET & SHARPENING STONE
__ CHAIN SAW, FUEL, OIL & TOOLS
__ SAW, SHOVEL, HAMMER & NAILS
__ CAMP LANTERN, FUEL & SPARE PARTS
__ CANDLE LANTERN &/OR CANDLES
__ WOOD STOVE & WOOD
__ GAS HEATER, FUEL & SPARE PARTS
__ STRIKERS, LIGHTERS & MATCHES
__ FOLDING TABLE & STOOLS
__ PORT-A-POTTI & TOILET PAPER

- CAMP SHOWER OR SUN SHOWER
- COMMUNICATIONS &/OR PUBLIC RADIO W/SPARE BATTERIES
- CAMP FLASHLIGHT & ALARM CLOCK
- LAND USE PERMIT
- CAMP TOOL KIT & FIRST AID KIT
- INSECT COILS & REPELLENT
- TAPE & TIE WIRE

COOKING & EATING

- CAMP STOVE, FUEL & SPARE PARTS
- COOK BOX OR STOVE STAND
- COOKING GRILL
- COOLER
- WATER PAIL OR JUG
- WATER PURIFIER
- COFFEE POT
- DUTCH OVEN
- FRYING PAN
- BOILING POTS
- 2-QUART DRINK CONTAINER
- SPATULA & LARGE SPOON
- COOK KNIFE
- CAN OPENER
- CUPS & PLATES
- TABLESPOONS, FORKS & TEASPOONS
- ALUMINUM FOIL
- PAPER TOWELS
- DISHWASHING TUB
- POT SCRUBBER/PAD & DISH SOAP
- PLASTIC TRASH BAGS

FOOD

(TOO VARIABLE TO LIST, COUNT MEALS NEEDED, ADD A LITTLE, AND MAKE SURE YOU HAVE ENOUGH EXTRA IN CASE OF WEATHER OR TRANSPORTATION DELAYS.)

CLOTHING

- SOCKS; LINERS & HEAVY DUTY
- SHORTS & T-SHIRTS
- LONG UNDERWEAR
- PANTS & SHIRTS
- VEST

Alaskan Camping 153

Kayak camping presents a specific set of gear requirements. Waterproof gear bags and minimal size/weight are top priorities.

__ COAT OR PARKA
__ WIND PANTS & COAT
__ RAIN GEAR
__ GLOVES, MITTENS & HATS
__ BELT &/OR SUSPENDERS
__ BOOTS, WADERS & CAMP SHOES
__ GAITERS
__ BANDANA

BACKPACKING
__ PACK FRAME & BAG
__ DAY &/OR FANNY PACK
__ ROPE, CORD &/OR TWINE
__ MAPS, COMPASS, GPS & PERSONAL ELT
__ FIRST AID KIT
__ INSECT REPELLENT
__ SPACE BLANKET & WHISTLE
__ WATER BOTTLE & SNACKS
__ FLASHLIGHT, EXTRA BATTERIES, BULB
__ LIGHTER, MATCHES, & FIRESTARTERS
__ CAMERA W/EXTRA FILM & BATTERIES
__ BINOCULARS

PERSONAL

__ TOWEL, WASH RAG & SOAP
__ TOOTHBRUSH, TOOTHPASTE & FLOSS
__ SHAVING KIT & COMB
__ TOILET PAPER & READING MATERIAL
__ PRESCRIPTION MEDICINE
__ EXTRA EYEGLASSES & CONTACTS
__ SUNGLASSES, SUNBLOCK
__ LIP BALM, ASPIRIN, & ANTACID
__ NEEDLE, THREAD & BUTTONS
__ CLIMBING POLE, EXTRA SHOELACES
__ DOG, DISH, FOOD, COLLAR, LEASH, BLANKET & WHISTLE

~

For those visitors who prefer a more comfortable Alaskan experience, there are numerous cruise boats to choose from. This one—the Discovery sailing out of Whittier—carries up to 12 passengers on first-class voyages throughout Prince William Sound.

CHAPTER EIGHT

FIREARMS/PROTECTION FOR VISITORS

Alaska has plenty of wild and sometimes dangerous animals. They are one of the big attractions to "The Last Frontier." Most visitors are somewhat apprehensive about getting too close to Alaska's wild animals, particularly predators like bears and wolves. Although there is some justification for these fears, visitors who know and follow just a few guidelines about Alaska's wildlife have very little to worry about.

BEARS

Both black and brown bears are commonly encountered by Alaskan visitors. Each year a few of these encounters become uncomfortable for man and beast. Adding a little understanding of these animals to a little common sense will help you avoid possibly dangerous situations.

Brown, grizzly and black bears have poor eyesight and keen noses. If they don't get your scent, they often have a hard time determining what you are, so they stand up to get a better look. This is not a threatening gesture, just a way to determine what you are. The vast majority of the time—over 99.99%—once they sense that you are human, they run. If a bear does stand up or come toward you, unless there is a tall, climbable tree nearby or a bear-proof shelter you can easily get to before the bear gets to you, do not run. Bears are very quick on their feet and you cannot outrun them. Running just indicates to them that you are afraid, so they might chase you to learn if you are a prey species or a smaller predator they can chase away. If you try to run and they catch you, the least they will do is slap you around a little to show you who's boss. If you resist, they will continue until you stop and they get tired of displaying their dominance.

If there is no safe retreat nearby and a bear comes toward you, the best thing to do is stand your ground and face the bear. Walk back and forth a few steps and yell to show the bear what you are. Usually (over 99% of the time) when a bear determines you are human, this is all he needs to know to decide that he should leave. If the bear still comes your way, you must stand your ground. Showing dominance among wild animals involves a lot of bluff behavior. Bears will often come within thirty feet and sometimes closer to test if they can bluff-charge you into backing down. If the only other option you have is to run, don't. I once had a brown bear run at me through heavy brush several times and then swerve away within thirty feet each time, trying to get me to run. He finally gave up his bluff and ran off. I had a rifle but wasn't about to use it until absolutely necessary. Whether or not it's true that *all* brown/grizzly bear charges are bluffs as some experts claim, I can't say for sure, but certainly the great majority of them are. In my 45 years of exploring the wilderness of Alaska, I have never had to shoot a bear— I don't think I've even come close—and I have spent upwards of 100 days in the field in many years.

The most serious threat from a brown/grizzly bear comes if you get too close to its kill or its young. In these cases there is often no time to react before the bear is upon you. For whatever reason, if a bear does attack you, the best thing to do is drop, curl into a ball and lie still. The bear may still hit you a couple times, but you have no choice at this point. Just wait until the bear leaves before moving.

Conversely, if you are attacked by a black bear, the best action to take varies with the situation. Black bears have been known to try to eat humans much more often than brown/grizzly bears, although it still happens much less than once per year for the entire state. The accepted strategy if black bears do attack is to stand and fight them off, making them go elsewhere for easier prey. There have been several cases of people fighting off black bears with

Firearms 157

Grizzly and brown bears are the most commonly feared Alaskan animals. They are large, dangerous creatures and should always be respected. However, they pose only a minimal threat to visitors who have some knowledge and use a little common sense.

only their fists by hitting their sensitive noses. A large stick would be much better if one is available. Black bears in most of Alaska average less than 200 lbs. so even on their hind feet they are shorter than the average man. However, if the bear is very large and you think it is only trying to chase you off, the best thing to do may be to lie still until it leaves–as you would if it were a brown/grizzly bear. The specific situation would determine your best course of action.

WOLVES AND OTHER CANINES

Wolves are still found in great numbers in Alaska and Canada but pose little threat to people. Because of their fear of humans and ability to stay out of sight, they are seldom seen even when abundant. However, coyotes and fox are common pests and steal whatever food they can. The only serious threat to people that any of these canines pose is their tendency to carry rabies. Any unusually friendly or strangely acting canine should be avoided and reported to authorities. Infected animals are highly contagious and unpredictable, so avoid any canine who acts unusual.

IN GENERAL

Alaska has other large animals which also should be treated with a little common sense and respect. Anytime you get between a wild animal and its young there is an element of danger. All females will defend their young vigorously, and large species like moose or caribou are capable of killing humans which threaten their young. Although caribou are generally not a problem because they keep their distance, moose have been known to kill humans while defending their calves. Adult moose can also kill a dog which gets too close. All big game animals should be treated with the respect that large, powerful animals with sharp hooves or claws deserve.

Other common sense behavior involves food. The first commandment is to never feed wild animals. People who do this should expect problems.

Bears catching and eating salmon on popular viewing streams in Alaska are sometimes habituated to humans. Sometimes they will allow people to get very close and then suddenly get protective or feel threatened–creating a very dangerous situation. Bears who hang around campgrounds, dumps and towns also pose a danger to people who get too close. Remember that wild animals are always that, no matter what situation you see them in. Treat them with respect, keep your distance, and always think safety first.

Campers in Alaska also need to take precautions with camp food. The best solution is to leave all food in a vehicle except at mealtime. The next best choice is to store all food high (a minimum of fifteen feet) up a tree. The last alternative if nothing else is available is to move all stored food a good distance away from camp–300 feet is reasonable. Bringing food into tents—particularly at night when bears are more active—is an open invitation to problems in bear country. Campers also need to be sure and keep a clean camp to keep food/garbage smells to a minimum.

Firearms 159

Moose are much more likely to be a threat to visitors than bears, partly because moose are much more common. Cow moose can weigh up to 1,000 lbs. and are very protective of their calves. Maintain a safe distance; watch for raised hackles, flattened ears and changes in mood; and always have a direction to retreat.

FIREARMS/PROTECTION

The first question to answer is whether or not you want to even consider bringing a firearm for protection. I strongly advise against it. It is unnecessary for over 99% of the adventures which visitors will have in Alaska. For the remaining 1%, I suggest you only bring a firearm if your experience with it, as well as your understanding of bears, is good enough that you aren't in more danger by having the firearm. Before you bring a firearm, you should consider:
•Canada arrests people who try to bring handguns across their borders.
•Canada now charges a fee for bringing rifles or shotguns across their borders.
•Firearms are not allowed in National Parks.

- Bears often bluff charge within ten yards. If you shoot a bear unnecessarily in Alaska, you may be fined and jailed.
- Firearms need constant maintenance in Alaska's wet weather or they will corrode, especially in the coastal areas.
- Having a firearm may convince you to take unnecessary chances with bears.
- There is a different strategy for shooting bears than there is for shooting any other wildlife. Do you know what it is?
- Bears will absorb an amazing amount of lead before they die.
- Once wounded, a bear is much more dangerous.
- Do you know the ten commandments of firearm safety?
- In thousands of days afield in Alaska, I have never had a bear attack me, and I have had only a few bluff charge me.

An alternative choice is to take pepper spray devices specifically designed to fend off bears. If they make you feel better, go ahead. My experience is that these devices aren't effective.

The best way to avoid wild animal problems in Alaska is to follow the advice of campground and tour personnel, guidelines in visitor handbooks (like this one) and your own common sense. I often say that people are much more likely to be maimed or injured in automobiles than by bears. About 40,000 people die each year in the U.S. in automobile accidents, about one person dies each year from a bear attack in Alaska–with 600,000 very outdoor-oriented residents and 1.2 million visitors each year. And that one person often is a hunter involved in a risky activity. Don't worry unnecessarily about our wildlife. Use common sense and enjoy it.

CHAPTER NINE

WATER QUALITY & FIRST AID

Water is *vital* to us. Our bodies are 60% water; our muscles are 70% water. The average person loses ten cups of water per day; an active backpacker can lose two or three times that amount. If we are dehydrated by only three percent, our muscles lose ten percent of their contractile strength; and our concentration, coordination, reaction time, and stamina are all impaired. Just a three percent dehydration also makes us more susceptible to hypothermia or heat stroke. Although most healthy people can last several weeks without food, three days without water can cause death. Because water is so important to our health and performance, we should all drink plenty of (safe) water.

OUR WATER NEEDS

A moderately active person will lose at least ten cups of water each day. Of this ten cups, three and one-half cups will be replaced from the food he or she eats—but this may be much less if the person is on a backpack hunt where drier, lighter-weight food is standard fare. Another half-cup of water is normally generated as a by-product of daily metabolism. The other six cups or more the person needs has to be replaced by drinking fluids; thus the recommendation for healthy people is to drink six to eight cups of water per day to avoid dehydration. An active person requires more than this minimum to perform at maximum capacity. Just one hour of strenuous hiking can require us to drink an extra four cups of water to remain fully hydrated.

Our body's thirst mechanism cannot keep up with its need for water. Thirst actually signals that our body is already slightly dehydrated. If we drink only in response to thirst, we only replace about half of what our bodies need to perform at 100% capacity. To compensate, we should drink fluids at the slightest indication of thirst and continue drinking a little more. By doing this, we can keep our bodies fully hydrated and perform at our maximum physical capacity.

Prolonged, strenuous physical exercise common to backpacking puts enormous demands on our bodies. This creates a need for large quantities of water to remove toxins from our bodies created as a result of this exertion, as well as to break down fats our bodies are using for energy. Re-hydration is most effective with cool (rather than warm) drinks within the first hour after exercise. Sports drinks (like Gatorade) also replace some of the electrolytes we lose and are absorbed faster than just plain water. Whether on a backpack trip to Alaska or just training for one, these sports drinks re-hydrate us better and will slightly enhance our performance. It is also a good way to simultaneously put carbohydrates into our systems.

A wise precaution to take on a backpacking trip is to have a water-carrying capacity of at least two quarts per person. If you know there is water available along your route, you can just carry the portion of these two quarts you will need until you reach the next water source. However, when uncertain about the next water source or traveling in unfamiliar country, it is always wise to carry extra water. I have run out of water only once, and I will never do it again. My partner and I were going back up a mountain to camp after a long day of climbing the mountains of Alaska. After just two hours of climbing without water, our mouths were so dry we couldn't swallow food to get more energy to continue. We were exhausted and had to bivouac on the mountainside overnight with no gear except our clothes. By morning we were mildly hypothermic; luckily for us it was early in the fall and not too cold.

When hiking in the mountains of Alaska you can often look ahead and plan your route to pass by water and replenish your supply. This may save carrying extra water or having to backtrack if you run out. Thinking ahead about water supplies is a mark of an experienced—and probably more successful—hiker.

Water Quality & First Aid 163

Even pristine waterfalls like this one in the Alaskan wilderness aren't necessarily safe sources of drinking water. To be absolutely safe, all water in Alaska should be chemically treated or filtered properly.

WATER QUALITY

The quality of your water supply is also very important. Unfortunately, there are basically no natural bodies of water that are not suspect as far as safety goes. Harmful concentrations of bacteria, viruses, or protozoans abound in 80-90% of the world's natural bodies of water. Even mountaintop springs in Alaska may make you ill.

One common protozoan everyone should be familiar with is called Giardia lamblia. It causes Giardiasis–popularly called "beaver fever" because of the typical mammalian carrier. It is commonly found downstream of beavers, but it also can be found upstream of any possible beaver habitat because it can be carried by other mammals as well. It is frequently contracted by visitors in Alaska and other remote lands where the water seems so (deceivingly) pristine. The diarrhea, loss of appetite, cramps, and nausea often don't appear for seven to ten days–which can be a blessing if the person has left the field by then and is back home closer to medical services. Even if the symptoms stop after a few days, the disease needs to be treated to prevent reoccurrences typical of this illness.

There are several ways to treat water to make it safe for drinking, but the most reliable is by boiling. Boiling for even one minute kills protozoans (preventing Giardiasis), viruses (hepatitis and polio viruses included), and bacteria. It is the one surefire method you can use to kill organisms if in doubt about the potability of any water source.

Another method of treating water is adding iodine. Iodine comes in tablet, crystal, or liquid form. Iodine is difficult to use because extreme care has to be taken to ensure every drop of water gets treated; it also gives the water a distinctive taste unpleasant to some people. Iodine does not kill the protozoan cryptosporidium, which is becoming more common in our water supplies.

There are also a wide array of compact filtering and/or purification systems designed for campers, hikers or fishermen requiring potable water in the field. They are available as just filtering devices, purifiers, or as systems that do both. There are many varieties and sizes which can meet the needs of any size group, from a single camper to a large camp with dozens of people. The better filtering devices are supposed to remove all bacteria and protozoans, but may not get all the viruses. The purifiers are better at removing the viruses, but don't always remove very small protozoans (like Giardia). A system which combines a filter with a purifier is thus, more reliable than either one alone. One advantage filtering systems and purifiers have over boiling is the ability to remove harmful, inorganic particulates—like heavy metals, chemicals, and other pollutants found in many urban areas. However, claims made about any water filter or purifier should be examined closely, as they are not always justifiable. Careful research should be done before buying to ensure a particular device will meet the person's needs.

Since most of my camping is done in Alaska and I don't have to worry too much about inorganic particulates, I usually rely on the boiling method to produce potable water. Of course, the other way to have enough safe drinking water is to always bring it with you. This is impractical when backpacking, but okay when you have transportation to your campsite or when on short day hikes.

Water Quality & First Aid

Drinking plenty of safe water is vital to good health, maximum performance and overall satisfaction with your Alaskan experience.

Regardless of how you get potable water when in the field, be sure and get enough of it. An ample water supply is vital to good health, maximum performance, and a safe trip. Successful hikers, campers and fisherman plan ahead to bring plenty of water, ensure there will be plenty of (safe) water available, or bring the means of producing enough water from available sources.

FIRST AID

Many Alaskan visitors participate in activities which can be dangerous. Fishing, boating, camping, wildlife viewing, etc. all entail some inherent risks. Alaskan visitors often seek out backcountry and wilderness locations hours or days away from medical assistance. These places are exactly what attract many of these visitors. As a result, basic first aid skills may be needed by any one of these visitors

First aid is the physical and emotional help given immediately to a victim of an injury or sudden illness. First aid classes are available from community schools, hospitals, clinics, nurses, private businesses, etc. for a nominal fee. Basic first aid and CPR (cardiopulminary resucitation) training classes are usually less than eight hours each. These skills are useful for everyone because any one of us may be the first person available to administer first aid in an emergency situation.

The following procedures should be carried out by trained medical personnel whenever available. Being able to recognize the urgency of a situation can sometimes mean the difference between life and death or permanent disability and full recovery. Other medical situations may not be urgent with plenty of time to wait for trained medical personnel; the best course of action may be to keep the victim warm, comfortable, and immobile until professional help can arrive. Basic first aid and CPR training can go a long way toward helping you properly evaluate and determine the proper course of action in many cases.

(Note: When ABCs are indicated in the following descriptions, this stands for Airway, Breathing, and Circulation. The first thing to do in a potentially serious medical situation is to clear and maintain the airway, check and restore breathing, and check and restore circulation—the three steps taught in a CPR class.)

Bleeding – Minor – Apply direct pressure with clean (sterile if possible) dressing, wash, clean with soap, apply ointment, tape closed. Major – Apply direct pressure with clean (sterile) dressing, elevate injury above heart, cover and/or tape edges together. Severe – Apply direct pressure with clean (sterile) dressing, elevate injury above heart. If bleeding stops, apply pressure bandage and tape. Use a tourniquet as a last resort because this will often result in loss of limb. Tourniquet = any tight band which constricts blood flow and is applied closer to the heart than the injury; can be made of belt, towel, or cloth band; loosen every 30 minutes for one minute, then reapply. If embedded object caused bleeding, leave it in unless it is very loose. Do not wiggle or remove; it will help stop bleeding if it is tight in the wound.

Broken Bones, Sprains – These are not easy to tell apart. Open fractures are obvious because bone protrudes through skin; pain, numbness and swelling occur. Treat open wound before splinting; check ABCs. Closed fractures: signs are pain, swelling, bluish color,

Water Quality & First Aid   167

and numbness. Splint area; use available padding and splint material to support joint on both sides of fracture. Elevate, use indirect ice pack (not on skin). <u>Sprains</u>: these are injuries to ligaments which cause pain, tenderness, swelling, and bluish color hours later. Splint limb and elevate above heart. Ice for 20 minutes hourly up to 72 hours.

Burns – <u>Minor</u> – Indicated by pain, reddened skin, and possibly blisters. Apply cool, running water immediately, dry, apply burn ointment if skin is unbroken, and cover with (sterile) bandage. <u>Major</u> – Indicated by white, charred skin. Use ABCs first if needed; wrap with clean, dry cloth; treat for shock (see **Shock** instructions).

Diarrhea – Usually from food poisoning or infection in intestinal tract. Frequent watery or even bloody stools, can be accompanied by nausea, vomiting and abdominal cramping. Severe dehydration can occur. Rest and plenty of fluids (Gatorade is good) and anti-diarrhetic like Immodium A-D if watery—not bloody—stools.

Frostbite – Discolored skin—white or gray, numbness. Immerse in <u>warm</u> water until area is soft or put area in armpits; do not rub or squeeze; do not use hot heat source. Do not thaw until danger of re-freezing is gone.

Heart Attack – Signs are chest discomfort like tightness or squeezing, mainly in center of chest; may spread to either shoulder, arm, neck or lower jaw. Usually lasts at least two minutes and may come and go. Accompanied by sweating, nausea, and shortness of breath. Use ABCs if unconscious. Have patient sit or lie down and rest.

Heat or Sun Stroke – Indicated by hot, dry skin–usually with no sweating, rapid breathing, dizziness, nausea, confusion, seizures, and/or unconsciousness. Get patient in shade, cool rapidly with water, ice, cold metal or rock–whatever you can find; give cool drinks if conscious. Yes, this is possible in Alaska. I know because I have been symptomatic myself. Remember, Alaska's sun is unusually hot.

Hypothermia – <u>Variable signs</u> – loss of judgement, loss of visual acuity, shivering, slurred speech, poor coordination, hallucinations, warm flashes, decreased limb function, and/or higher

Alaskan experiences are often in remote locations, far from medical assistance. Knowing basic first aid can be a comforting feeling and make these vacations less stressful, and more enjoyable for everyone.

Water Quality & First Aid   169

blood pressure and pulse at first followed by depressed blood pressure and pulse. <u>Mild Hypothermia treatment</u> – Place victim in warm environment, exercise to warm, give food and warm liquids, apply heat packs, give warm bath or shower if alert, or get skin-to-skin contact with a warm body in a sleeping bag. <u>Severe Hypothermia treatment</u> – Treat as for mild hypothermia if pulse and breathing are present, but do not give warm bath or shower. Do not give anything by mouth, and do not exercise victim. If pulse and breathing are absent for 45 seconds, start CPR.

Bee Stings – Allergic reactions are facial swelling, difficulty breathing, or signs of shock. Allergic persons should have bee sting kit. They need epinephrine as soon as possible. Non-allergic victims just suffer minor pain. Remove stinger with outward scraping motion using fingernail or knife; do not squeeze stinger or attached sac because this may drive venom into victim. Clean area; use ice or cool water to soothe; baking soda paste may ease pain.

Neck & Head Injuries – <u>Neck Fracture</u> indicated by stiff or painful neck, inability to move limbs or any body parts, or tingling sensation. Treatment is to immobilize head and neck with padding and splint and, *moving victim very carefully*, slide victim onto body-size board and tie to board. <u>Head Injury</u> – Indicated by scalp wound, skull fracture, blood from nose–mouth–ears, unconsciousness, headache, vomiting, convulsions, or different-sized pupils. Treatment is ABCs first, then immobilize head and neck, keep warm, treat gently, victim should lie down; treat for shock.

Poisoning – <u>External</u> – Acids, bases, solvents or poison plants; flush with water at least 15–20 minutes. <u>Internal</u> – Do not cause vomiting unless sure it was not caustic. Treatment is ABCs, then CPR.

Shock – This is a secondary condition resulting from trauma or injury and is life-threatening. Symptoms are anxiety, thirst, sweating, paleness, rapid or weak pulse, dizziness, or unconsciousness. It often results in death if not treated immediately. Treatment is ABCs, then CPR; handle victim gently, have victim lie down, keep warm, elevate feet 15 inches unless neck injury or other broken bones and reassure patient. If unconscious and no neck or head injury or broken bones, place victim face down with head to one side.

Stroke – Caused by lack of blood circulation to brain; indicated by loss of or trouble with speech, dizziness or loss of consciousness; weakness or numbness in arm, leg, or one side of face; or trouble with vision in one eye. Treatment is ABCs.

In addition to giving you the *ability* to administer life-saving first aid should the situation arise, a *knowledge* of first aid builds confidence in your self-sufficiency as travelers and just everyday people. Travelers with this type of confidence are more able to enjoy themselves in remote areas where safety is an important concern. These remote areas–like Alaska–often present unique experiences, which may not be enjoyed by others who, for fear of medical situations, stay closer to civilization.

Having the right clothing and gear can make an Alaskan visit not only more enjoyable, but much safer. This smiling visitor has knee-high rubber boots, sunglasses, a watch cap, a waterproof jacket and a fleece liner–all good gear for a comfortable Alaskan experience.

CHAPTER TEN

CLOTHING & GEAR RECOMMENDATIONS FOR ALASKAN DESTINATIONS

This chapter has my recommendations for specific brand names and models of clothing and equipment to buy for your visit. I chose Cabela's as the main source of these items for several reasons:

•Convenience–You can buy everything you need for your Alaskan visit from this one source.

•Quality–Cabela's clothing and gear are high-quality items that I use personally and can honestly recommend.

•Shopping Options–Cabela's has frequently published catalogs, an on-line store and several walk-in stores to satisfy all types of shoppers.

•Women's and children's sizes are available in many items, plus a *separate women's section* with clothing designed just for them.

•Variety of Brands–Cabela's offers their brand as well as other well-known brand items to choose from.

•Price–Cabela's offers good merchandise at very good prices. They even offer a Cabela's Visa Card which returns 1% to 2% for every dollar you charge on it.

These are the same reasons I personally use Cabela's merchandise. I chose Cabela's without any incentive from the company. I did request a computer disk with scanned images of some of their merchandise and that is the only thing they supplied for this book. Neither Cabela's nor I have made any other commitments to each other.

People often forget to consider their pets' comfort when they come to Alaska. Pets who are unaccustomed to cold, wet weather can also suffer from hypothermia, just like people. An inexpensive dog vest—like this one from Cabela's—is a great way to ensure your canine friend also enjoys his visit.

The recommended items in this chapter are accompanied by short descriptions and sometimes by photos. You can find some of the non-Cabela's items at other sources–both catalogs and stores. At the end of this chapter is a list of some of the other catalogs and stores which I use in addition to Cabela's. You may well find similar items at these other sources with slight differences (maybe price) which appeal to you. Although I do feel Cabela's is the best single source of Alaska wear, there are, of course, other places to find good clothing and gear.

BASE LAYER

The base layer of clothing lies next to your skin. The base layer consists of underwear tops and bottoms, long underwear if necessary and socks. The base layer should feel comfortable to your skin and keep it dry.

For many inactive or mildly active Alaskan experiences, cotton or silk underwear and socks work fine. As long as you are not perspiring which would dampen a cotton or silk base layer and eventually chill you, these materials are fine. Cotton underwear and socks are available almost anywhere clothing is sold.

Clothing and Gear Recommendations 173

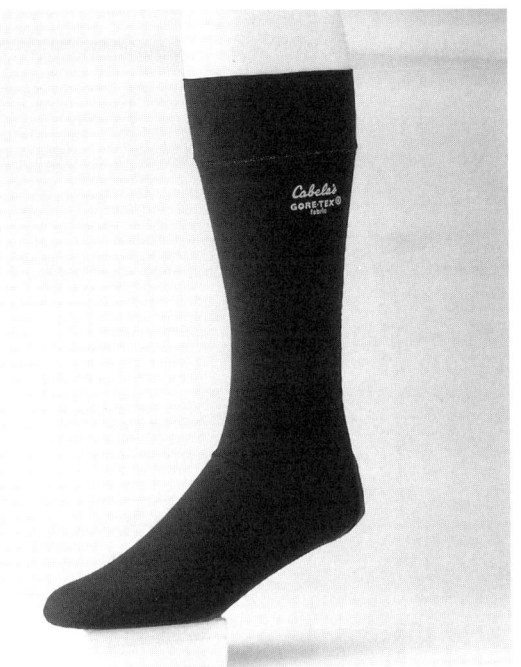

These GoreTex Oversocks from Cabela's are great for keeping your feet dry in the wettest conditions.

Recommendation #1: Cabela's Silk and Silk/Wool Blend Underwear and Silk Accessories: Long underwear bottoms, tops, sock liners, glove liners, and dickies for men and women. Comfortable next to the skin and machine washable. **Recommended for: any season or destination in Alaska as long as the activity level is low so you won't be perspiring.** **Source: Cabela's**

For any activity where you will be perspiring, I recommend synthetic base layers. Synthetic underwear and socks will actually wick moisture away from your skin, keeping you dry and warm.

Recommendation #2: Cabela's MTP (Maximum Thermal Protection) Performance Underwear with ScentEliminator™: Synthetic briefs, boxers and crew-neck t-shirts which wick moisture away from the skin faster than other synthetics. The soft fabric is comfortable and is modified to permanently inhibit the growth of bacteria and odors. **Recommended for: all seasons in Alaska and any activity where you may perspire.** **Source: Cabela's**

Recommendation #3: Cabela's Thermax, Thermastat, or MTP long underwear: These three synthetic materials all offer the moisture-wicking properties important to staying dry and warm in cool or cold temperatures. They come in three different weights for more warmth when needed. Lightweight two piece suits for cool weather or heavyweight one-piece suits for really cold conditions. Available in men's and women's styles. **Recommended as base or insulating layer for**: cruises/boating/rafting/kayaking/boat fishing anytime; any trip north of the Arctic Circle any time of year; mountain backpacking any time–lighter weight thermals in summer, heavier models in spring and fall; any light aircraft rides; railroad trips in fall, winter or spring. *I personally have two sets of these.* **Source: Cabela's**

Recommendation #4: ThorLo™ Socks: Synthetic socks, sometimes with a little wool added, made of high-bulk Orlon. They come in dozens of styles and weights and keep your feet very dry and very comfortable. **Recommended for:** every activity you do–wherever and whenever you do it. Great socks. *I personally wear these 99% of the time.* **Source: REI, Sports Authority, Campmor (see page 108 for photo)**

SECOND OR INSULATING LAYER

The second layer is sometimes the outer layer of clothing when weather permits. More often in Alaska, the second layer is used to insulate us and a protective layer will be worn outside of this one. There may be from one to several insulating layers, depending on the weather. This layer may consist of long underwear, shirts, vests, sweaters or light jackets.

Recommendation #5: Cabela's GoreTex™ Stretch Oversocks: Waterproof, breathable, stretch socks keep your feet dry even in wet boots. **Recommended for:** any activity where your footwear may leak, especially on long hikes, anytime in Alaska. *I personally have a pair of these.* **Source: Cabela's (see page 173 for photo)**

Recommendation #6: Cabela's Chamois or Stonewash Shirts: Comfortable cotton shirts. **Recommended for:** outer wear when conditions are dry or as insulating layer under raingear; use anytime as an insulating layer when your shirt won't get wet from perspiration or precipitation; –men's and women's styles. **Source: Cabela's**

Clothing and Gear Recommendations 175

This Cabela's Worsterlon shirt is one of the best shirts made. The material is windproof, water-resistant, fast-drying, comfortable, durable and doesn't wrinkle. Everyone should have at least two or three of these for wear in Alaska or anywhere you need a long-sleeve shirt.

Recommendation #7: Cabela's Polartek™ Microfleece or Wind Pro Shirts and Pants: Wind and water-resistant shirts and pants are very comfortable and dry quickly. **Recommended for:** an outer layer on summer days or an insulating layer on cooler days anytime in Alaska; particularly useful when camping or backpacking to keep you warm in wet conditions. **Source: Cabela's**

Recommendation #8: Cabela's Trek-Tech Sweaters with WindStopper®: Synthetic wind-blocking sweaters. **Recommended for:** use as an insulating layer on board any ship, boat, raft or kayak or when exploring cities in cool temperatures; cool fishing or hiking trips any time of year anywhere in Alaska; for an insulating layer in winter. **Source: Cabela's**

Recommendation #9: Cabela's Worsterlon Shirts: Synthetic shirts which are very tough and wind, water and wrinkle-resistant. **Recommended for:** everything you do and anywhere you go; great shirts for traveling because they look good, don't wrinkle and are very comfortable. *I personally think these shirts are the best for* *almost any activity which requires a long-sleeve shirt.* **Source: Cabela's**

Recommendation #10: Cabela's Canvas Zip-Off Pants or 7-Pocket Hiker Pants & Shorts: Canvas pants and shorts for comfort and versatility. **Recommended for:** summer use when sun is a possibility, but you are never far from your raingear and dry clothes; not for backpacking (these are cotton) or any remote trips unless you also carry synthetic pants if the weather turns cold or wet; –men's, women's and children's sizes. **Source: Cabela's**

Recommendation #11: Sporthill Koch XC 3SP Pants: Synthetic stretch, wind and water-resistant pants. **Recommended for:** backpacking, camping, hiking, climbing and skiing in any weather; use as an outer layer in mild weather and an insulating layer in cold weather. *I personally use a pair of these pants 50-100 days per year.* **Source: REI or Barney's Sports Chalet** (Anchorage)

Recommendation #12: Cabela's Polartec™ 200 or 300 Jacket, Vest and Pants: Fleece clothing which is warm, water-resistant and dries quickly, but not wind-proof. **Recommended for:** as an outer layer on mild days without wind; best used for an insulating layer on cool to the coldest days; good for anytime except the warmest summer days in Alaska. **Source: Cabela's**

Recommendation #13: Wilson or Woolrich Wool Pants, Bibs, Shirts and Coats: Traditional wool clothing for warmth and durability. **Recommended for:** warmth when weight doesn't matter and clothing can be dried as needed; good for any boat rides when it can be very chilly; good for sitting outdoors in cool temperatures–like fishing from a boat; use as insulating or outer layer anytime of year in Alaska. *I personally have about a dozen wool shirts, pants and coats.* **Source: Cabela's, L.L. Bean, Dunn's**

OUTER OR PROTECTIVE LAYER

Most of these items are designed to be the outer layer of clothing. Some can be used as an insulating layer in colder weather. The water-resistant items are okay in many of Alaska's light drizzles, but wouldn't keep you dry in sustained rains. Look for the waterproof items for the most protection from the really wet weather Alaska often provides. If you don't bring any other rain protec-

Clothing and Gear Recommendations 177

tion, as the minimum I suggest everyone visiting Alaska has one waterproof, hooded jacket. Protective layers can be pants, coats, jackets, parkas, rainwear, windbreakers, caps, hats, gloves, mittens and footwear.

Recommendation #14: Cabela's Original Northern Lite Three-Season Jacket **or WindStopper Jackets, Hooded Jackets and Pants:** Water-resistant clothing made of warm fleece. **Recommended for:** spring through fall in all areas of Alaska except the Arctic; any of these items can be used as an insulating layer in very cold or very wet weather; jackets are good for exploring seaside cities in cool weather with or without light rain. **Source:** Cabela's (see photo, page 178)

Recommendation #15: Cabela's Lightweight Jacket with Goosedown or Primaloft: light jacket of warm goosedown or water-resistant Primaloft. **Recommended for:** an insulating layer–goosedown jacket in cold, dry winter weather–Primaloft jacket for winter or wetter times of year. *I personally use one of these coats regularly in spring or fall weather.* **Source:** Cabela's

Recommendation #16: Cabela's Packable Nylon Rain Gear: Lightweight, polyurethane-coated rain pants, coats and bibs. **Recommended for:** rain protection at any temperature down to freezing; a good item to have to keep all the rain off your clothes for up to several hours at a time. Compact size makes these convenient to carry at all times. **Source:** Cabela's

These WindStopper pants from Cabela's are windproof, water-resistant, lightweight and very comfortable. They can be used for a protective layer, or for an insulating layer on colder days.

Recommendation #17: Cabela's Ultimate GoreTex Systems Parka and Bibs: Rainwear with zip-in jacket liner for really cold weather.

Cabela's Northern Lite Three-Season Jacket would be a good outer layer on windy, cool days around the water or used as an insulating layer on cold winter days. The outer shell repels water well and the inner layer of fleece is comfortable. It's also stylish enough to wear traveling or around town.

Recommended for: any spring or fall trips; cold summer fishing trips, with the bibs; useful whenever temperature may be near freezing but rain is still a possibility. **Source: Cabela's**

Recommendation #18: Cabela's Premium II GoreTex Parka & Pants: Waterproof, breathable rainwear. **Recommended for:** cool weather trips where rain is likely; good for wind and waterproof layer on board cruise ships or any type of boat; a warm, waterproof, general-purpose coat good for any above-freezing Alaskan experience; –men's and women's styles. **Source: Cabela's (see page 189 for photo)**

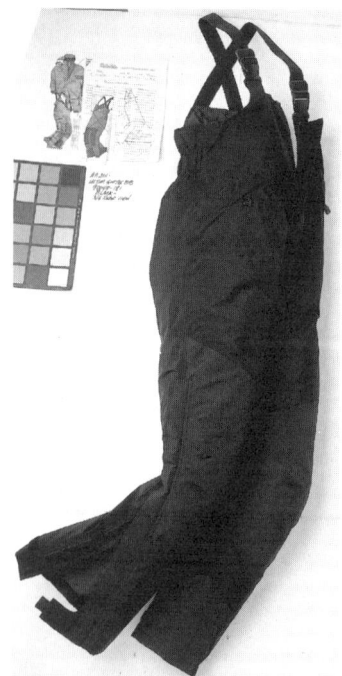

Cabela's Ultimate GoreTex Systems Bibs–for sitting in cool weather.

****A WATERPROOF, GORETEX, HOODED JACKET LIKE #17 OR #18 (above) IS ONE OF MY MOST HIGHLY RECOMMENDED ITEMS FOR ANY ALASKAN VISITOR. IT

Clothing and Gear Recommendations

WILL DO MORE TO KEEP YOU COMFORTABLE IN ALASKA THAN ANY OTHER ONE ITEM IN THIS BOOK.****

Recommendation #19: Cabela's Dry-Plus™ Mountain Parka with Thinsulate or Goose Down: Waterproof, cold-weather parka. **Recommended for:** cold weather trips when temperature dips no lower than 20° F or cool, windy days on the water or seaside areas with wind; Alaska Peninsula anytime of year; Denali Park trips in May or August; early or late fishing trips; – men's and women's sizes. **Source:** Cabela's

The Cabela's Dry-Plus™ Mountain Parka is waterproof, wind-proof, and warm enough for light winter wear or on really cold days on the water. Good for fishing from boats when you will have to sit still for long periods.

Recommendation #20: Cabela's Everest Down Parka: Down-filled, cold-weather, hooded parka. **Recommended for:** cold weather from fall to spring; you may need additional clothing for the very cold weather of Alaska's winters anywhere north of Anchorage; not recommended for wet weather. **Source:** Cabela's

Recommendation #21: Outdoor Research Ice Cap'd: Water and wind-resistant ball cap style hat with hidden earflaps. **Recommended for:** general use hat for Alaska from spring through fall; some warmth and water resistance with style while on boats or walking city streets. **Source:** Cabela's

Cabela's Trans-Alaska Hat is a good style to carry for mild to cold conditions.

Recommendation #22: Cabela's Trans-Alaska Hat: Waterproof, wind-proof, and lined with pile for warmth, these hats have bills and earflaps. **Recommended for:** cold summer boating trips anywhere in Alaska; any spring or fall outdoor activities over two hours anywhere south of Brooks Range; light-duty hat for less-severe winter temperatures; backpacking or camping trips from spring to fall. **Source: Cabela's**

Recommendation #23: WindStopper Fleece Balaclava: Windproof head and neck protection in cold weather. **Recommended for:** backpacking, camping, fishing or other outings of several hours on cool, wet, or windy days anytime of year; base layer when snowmachining or dog mushing; sea kayaking or small boat trips in cool weather. **Source: Cabela's, other sporting goods stores**

Recommendation #24: Cabela's GoreTex/Thinsulate Gloves and Mittens: Waterproof, windproof, insulated hand-wear with elastic cuffs to keep out snow and water. **Recommended for:** cold days boating or fishing or even on deck of ferries and ships; anytime you sit or stand in cool weather; -in men's and women's sizes. **Source: Cabela's, other sporting goods stores**

Cabela's GoreTex/Thinsulate Mittens

Recommendation #25: StormKloth Gloves: Waterproof, windproof, breathable, fast-drying lightweight gloves. **Recommended for:** anytime you might get chilly and/or wet hands–which is anytime and anywhere in Alaska; a great item to have on any trip just in case; great for backpacking, fishing, camping or just sight-seeing–even within city limits. **Source: Cabela's, other sporting goods stores**

FOOTWEAR

There are literally hundreds of styles and makes of good footwear, and just as many bad ones. I could fill a whole book with an

Clothing and Gear Recommendations 181

in-depth analysis of gear for your feet. However, people's feet vary as much as people so I believe you should try shoes on before buying them. I can tell you what I think is a great shoe because of the design, but if it doesn't feel comfortable you should look for another brand with a similar design which does feel right. Cabela's does have a full refund policy so you can return any footwear which doesn't fit. They also have several stores where you can actually go to try on their footwear. And some of the styles I recommend are actually other brand names so you can probably find them at other stores in your area. You can also get the full description of the footwear I am recommending (from Cabela's catalog) and then take it with you when you go shopping for footwear. By comparing footwear designs, you should be able to find shoes or boots very similar to the ones I have recommended.

Recommendation #26: New Balance Country Walker, for Men and Women: Waterproof, leather walking shoes suitable for street or trail with Abzorb® inserts for comfort. **Recommended for:** a great knock-around shoe for any trip to Alaska; keeping your feet dry in comfort and style. *I personally use these shoes.* **Source: Cabela's, REI, shoe stores (see page 103 for photo)**

Recommendation #27 Rocky® Baseball Stitch GoreTex® Oxford & Chukka: Waterproof, high or low-top, lightly-treaded, multipurpose shoes with style. **Recommended for :** another great all-purpose shoe to keep you dry and warm in style during most Alaskan experiences; low-tops for city use, high-tops for light hiking–but neither suited to backpacking or serious hiking. **Source: Cabela's, other shoe stores**

Recommendation #28: Cabela's Professional Outdoor Footwear: Seven styles of rubber bottom/leather top footwear made for the Alaskan climate. Moccasin style up to 12" boot. **Recommended for:** one of the best styles for Alaskan trips; moccasin slip-ons for relaxing at night or 12" boot for really wet conditions; these will keep your feet dry in Alaska. *I personally use a pair of these.* **Source: Cabela's**

Recommendation #29: Cabela's Outfitter Series GoreTex® Insulated or Uninsulated Boots: Hiking boots with leather uppers, lug soles, GoreTex lining, -with or without insulation. **Recommended for:** hiking, camping, wet boat decks or even city streets in winter time; any cool excursions which might also be wet. **Source: Cabela's**

Recommendation #30: Cabela's or LaCrosse Knee-High Rubber Boots: Knee-high rubber boots with or without insulation. **Recommended for:** wet weather–July through October in Alaska; Southeast Alaska where they are called "Ketchikan Sneakers" because residents there wear these; fishing trips–on boats or on shore. **Source: Cabela's**

Recommendation #31: Rocky Winter Rec Boots: Waterproof, insulated light winter boot. **Recommended for:** city use in winter; cruise ships or fishing boats in wet and/or cool weather; -in men's and women's sizes. **Source: Cabela's**

Recommendation #32: Sorel® Glacier: Winter boot with rubber bottom, nylon top and insulation for extreme cold. **Recommended for:** winter in Alaska–down to below zero. **Source: Cabela's, other sporting goods stores**

Cabela's Trans-Alaska II Boot–for really cold Alaskan visits.

Recommendation #33: Cabela's Trans-Alaska II Boot: Extreme weather boot. **Recommended for:** extreme cold of Alaska's winters; Iditarod viewing–especially in Nome; dog-mushing or snowmachine riding. **Source: Cabela's**

LUGGAGE AND DUFFEL

Recommendation #34: Alaskan Guide Model Expedition Ballistic Bags: Tough, stylish duffels in many sizes. **Recommended for:** all Alaskan travel. **Source: Cabela's**

Recommendation #35: Cabela's Ripcord II Duffel

Clothing and Gear Recommendations 183

Bags: Tough, waterproof, basic duffel bags with optional backpacking straps. **Recommended for:** all Alaskan travel at minimal cost. **Source:** Cabela's

Recommendation #36: Cabela's Boundary Waters II Bags: Heavy-duty, coated PVC, waterproof bags for wet conditions; some with backpacking straps. **Recommended for:** kayaking trips; remote travel on small boats or aircraft; camping. **Source:** Cabela's

CAMPING, BACKPACKING AND MISCELLANEOUS GEAR

Recommendation #37: Cabela's Alaskan Guide Model® Tents: Two to eight-person, geodesic dome tents with waterproof floors and flys. Designed to shed wind and rain. **Recommended for:** camping where weight is not crucial in moderate conditions of spring through fall in Alaska. **Source:** Cabela's (see page 188 for photo)

Cabela's Boundary Waters II Bags (or this older version) are great for insuring your extra clothes and gear will be dry.

Recommendation #38: Trekker V™ Sleeping Bags: Quallofil®-filled, water-resistant, lightweight mummy and rectangular bags at a good price for temperatures from 50° F to -20° F. **Recommended for:** camping, backpacking or anytime a sleeping bag is required in Alaska. **Source:** Cabela's

Recommendation #39: Cabela's Summit Sleeping Bags: Hollofil®II-filled, water-resistant, roomy bags. **Recommended for:** Alaskan camping or any trip a bag is needed where weight is not a concern. **Source:** Cabela's

Cabela's Trans-Alaska™ Sleeping Bag for really cold conditions when weight is also a concern.

Recommendation #40: Cabela's Trans-Alaska™ Sleeping Bag: Down and Polarguard®-filled bag for really cold trips always below freezing, when weight is a concern. **Recommended for:** any cold trips in Alaska down to well below zero; cool-weather trips in Alaska where a bag is required and you have a hard time staying warm in average bags; not for wet weather. **Source: Cabela's**

Recommendation #41: Cabela's Self-Inflating Sleeping Pads: Foam-filled, durable, self-inflating pads for comfortable nights. **Recommended for:** any temperature where you need a pad and comfort is more important than weight. **Source: Cabela's (see page 185 for photo)**

Recommendation #42: Ridge-Rest® or Z-Rest® Sleeping Mats: Comfortable, compact, lightweight, closed-cell pads provide lots of comfort for backpacking or camping. **Recommended for:** backpacking, camping, or anytime weight and size need to be kept to minimum while still being comfortable. **Source: Cabela's, REI, sporting goods stores**

Recommendation #43: Cabela's Alaskan Pack Frames and Backpacks: Lightweight, durable, large-capacity packs and bags with sternum straps and padded hip belts. **Recommended for:** backpacking anywhere and any time in Alaska. **Source: Cabela's**

Recommendation #44: PUR® Water Purifiers and Water Filters: Small to large size water cleansing systems. **Recommended for:**

Clothing and Gear Recommendations 185

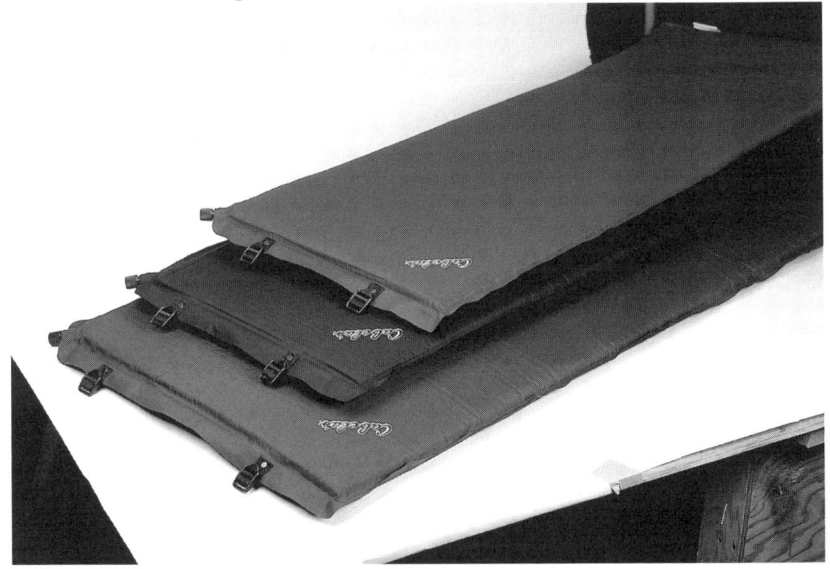

Cabela's Self-Inflating Sleeping Pads for comfortable sleeping when weight is not the main concern.

anyone who visits remote areas of Alaska and will need to supply their own drinking water. **Source: Cabela's**

Recommendation #45: Garmin 12XL GPS: Tough, reliable GPS units for backcountry travel. **Recommended for:** anyone who plans to travel off-road in Alaska. **Source: Cabela's, other sporting goods stores**

Recommendation #46: Cabela's Waterproof Binoculars: Multi-coated, rubber-armored, compact and full-size binoculars with 30-day satisfaction guarantee. **Recommended for:** any sight-seeing, wildlife viewing, backpacking, cruise trips, camping, etc. in Alaska. **Source: Cabela's (see page 119 for photo)**

Recommendation #47: Cabela's 5mm Neoprene Dog Vest: Neoprene dog vests for warmth, protection, safety and flotation. **Recommended for:** any medium to extra large dogs which may not be accustomed to the temperatures or cold water of Alaska; anytime of year. **Source: Cabela's**

Recommendation #48: Disposable Hand or Body Warmers: External Heat Source for any outdoor activity. **Recommended for:** any time you feel cold. Inexpensive, compact and they feel great in your pocket, boot, or especially in the back waistband of your

pants–which is where they do the most good. Highly recommended
Source: Most outdoor stores, also variety stores in Alaska (see page 188 for photo)

Those are my recommendations for Alaska wear. You could put together a comfortable Alaskan wardrobe solely from this list or solely from a Cabela's catalog. If you would like to expand the list of items, you can apply the analyses presented in earlier chapters as you shop other sources for clothing and gear. The following are good sources for Alaskan clothing and gear.

SOURCES OF CLOTHING & GEAR

CABELA'S
One Cabela Drive
Sidney, NE 69160-9555
1-800-237-4444
www.cabelas.com

Bass Pro Shops
2500 E. Kearney
Springfield, MO 65898-0123
1-800-227-7776
www.basspro.com

Campmor
P.O. Box 700-P
Saddle River, New Jersey 07458-0700
1-800-226-7667
www.campmor.com

Dunn's
P.O Box 406
Greenville, NC 27835
1-800-353-8621
www.dunnscatalog.com

L.L. Bean
Freeport, Maine 04033-0001
1-800-221-4221
www.llbean.com

Clothing and Gear Recommendations

The North Face
2013 Farallon Drive
San Leandro, CA 94577
www.thenorthface.com

REI
1700 45th Street East
Sumner, WA 98390
1-800-426-4840
www.rei.com

Sierra Trading Post
5025 Campstool Road
Cheyenne, WY 82007-1898
1-800-713-4534
www.sierratradingpost.com

The Sportsman's Guide
411 Farwell Ave
So. St. Paul, MN 55075-0239
1-800-888-3006
www.sportsmansguide.com

ALASKAN STORES

Barney's Sports Chalet
906 W. Northern Lights Blvd.
Anchorage, AK 99503
907-561-5242

Chimo Guns
501 E. Herning Ave.
Wasilla, AK 99654
907-376-5261

Mountain View Sports Center
3838 Old Seward Highway
Anchorage, AK 99503
907-563-8600

Cabela's Alaskan Guide Model® Tents are dome-shaped to shed the wind and designed to keep you comfortable in Alaska. They come in sizes from 2-person up to 8-person. They also come with either fiberglass or aluminum poles. They are not for backpacking because of their weight, but they are built to be sturdy.

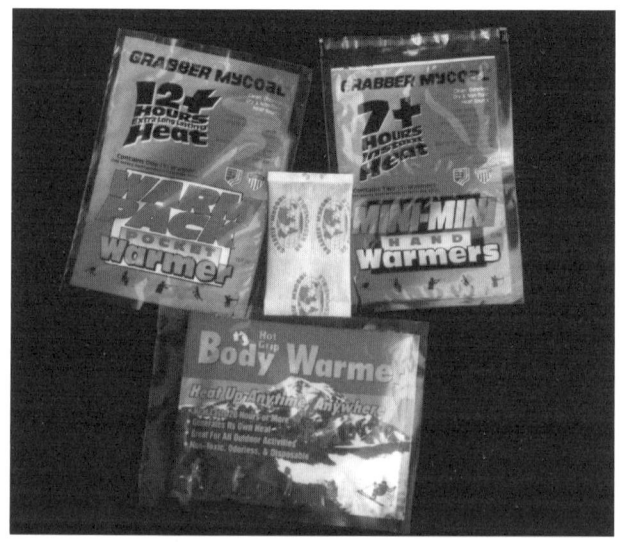

Disposable handwarmers are one item no one who worries about cold in Alaska should be without. They are small, inexpensive and really warm for 7 to 20 hours– depending on which ones you buy.

Clothing and Gear Recommendations 189

Cabela's Premium II GoreTex Parka is waterproof, breathable rainwear to keep you warm, dry and comfortable in wet and/or cool weather. A good parka for spring through fall if it is not too cold. For colder conditons, wear insulating layers under this parka.

This Glacier Peak Gore-Tex® Parka by Sportif USA is another variety of waterproof, wind-resistant jacket which is very useful in Alaska. Available from Sierra Trading Post.

If you bring clothing and gear which insulates, is waterproof and stops the wind, you will be comfortable on your Alaskan visit.

CONCLUSION

Alaska is a fragile land. Most of Alaska experiences a short growing season and a long winter. The plants and wildlife have to do all of their growing and recovering during the short summer. The long winters are a time of trying to just survive until spring. Any damage done to the living ecosystems sets the organisms back a little in their struggle to make it in a harsh environment. Ample evidence of these setbacks which haven't been overcome is visible in the scars left on the tundra in almost every area of Alaska.

Lichens which make up a part of the tundra can be as much as fifty years old and only one inch tall. Trees in our forests may be one hundred years old but only eight inches thick. Some wildlife populations also have unbelievably slow growth rates because of our harsh environment. Plants and wildlife populations which grow slowly cannot easily recover from damage during any season and particularly not from significant setbacks during the short summer growing season.

Alaska has about 600,000 residents. The state currently receives about 1.2 million visitors per year–most of those coming from mid-May through mid-September. This means that twice as many visitors as residents have an opportunity to affect the Alaskan ecosystems and the environment. As a lifelong Alaskan who loves this state and intends to stay indefinitely, I am asking you to take care of this wonderful place during your visits. I don't mean we can't harvest the forests, catch the fish, hunt the game or travel over Alaska in search of great experiences. These are all renewable natural resources which should be used for man's benefit. I'm only asking that you take care as you visit and enjoy Alaska. Please don't do any damage to its fish, wildlife or any part of the ecosystems which isn't necessary. It takes longer for our land to recover than in most environments. We should use our land to benefit man as much as possible. But, if we are good stewards of the land, more will be possible for us and everything else which lives here.

Index

Symbols

3SP 91, 176

A

Alaska Marine Highway 76
Alaska Oil Pipeline 74
Alaska Peninsula
    25, 27, 42, 56, 95, 107, 179
Alaska Range 62
Alaskan camping 125
Alaska's Banana Belt 70
Alaska's sun 13
Anchor Point 49
Anchorage 15, 27, 34
Anderson 63
Aniak 39
ANTLER CARVINGS 198
    Sheep horn carvings 198
Arctic 25, 26
Arctic Circle 26, 31, 40, 174
Arctic Ocean 36, 68, 69
Arctic region 26
Aurora Borealis 26, 32
auto-focusing camera 114
average wind speed 30

B

Baranof Island 70
Barney's Sports Chalet 176, 187
Barrow 12, 26, 36
base layer 90, 95, 172
Bass Pro Shops 186
bathtub style 129
bears 155, 157
Bering Sea 38, 42
Bering Sea Coast 26
Bethel 26, 38
Bettles 26, 40
binoculars 111, 117
    cleaning optics 119
    Compact binoculars 118
    Rubber armored binos 119
    waterproof binoculars 185
break-in process 104
Bristol Bay 56
Brooks Range 26, 40
bug index 33

C

Cabela's
    119, 150, 171, 172, 174, 176, 177,
    179, 182, 184, 185, 186
cameras 111
camp stove 139
    backpacking stove 140
    stove fuel 140
Campmor 174, 186
Cantwell 63
canvas 126, 176
    coated canvas fabric 126
Chena Hot Springs 45
Chickaloon 67
Chilkoot Trail 91
Chimo Guns 187
chinook winds 44
    Chinooks 39
Chitina 46
Chugach Mountains 34, 46, 74
Clam Gulch 52
clothing & gear recommendations
    171
clothing characteristics 85
Coast Mountains 50
Cold Bay 27, 42
compass 142, 143
composition 112, 113
conduction 79, 80
convection 79
Cook Inlet 34, 48, 66
Coolmax 90

Copper Center 46
Cordova 75
cordura nylon 126
cotton 86, 172, 174
Craig 54

D

daylight on 15th 30
Delta Junction 45
Denali National Park 62, 179
  Denali 63
Dillingham 57
Discovery Voyages
  Discovery 4, 123, 154
disposable camera 115
disposable handwarmers 107
  disposable hand warmers
    185, 188
Douglas Island 51
Dry-Plus 93, 179
duffel bags 122, 126, 183
Dunn's 176, 186

E

ecosystems 191
Emergency Locator Transmitter 145
environment 191
evaporation 79, 81, 86

F

fabrics 86
Fairbanks 26, 32, 44, 60
firearms 155, 159
first aid 161, 165, 168
first aid kit 148
fleece 90, 170, 176, 178
foot medicine 110
footwear 101, 103, 106, 180
fragile land 191

G

gear checklist 151

Giardia lamblia 163
  Giardia 164
glacier 80, 85
  river of ice 80
Glennallen 46
GoreTex 93, 94, 101, 130
GoreTex socks 108
GPS 144, 185
Gulf Coast 25, 27
Gulf of Alaska 48, 50, 58, 72
Gulkana 27, 46

H

Haines 51
hard-sided luggage 121
Healy 63
heat retention 81
heat transfer 79
Hollowfill 92
Homer 48
Hoonah 51
horizontal rain 27, 54, 57
Houston 67
humidity 30
hypothermia
  80, 81, 82, 87, 89, 92, 96, 161

I

ice-fog 60
Iditarod 64, 65, 96, 106
  The Last Great Race 64
Inside Passageway 76
insulating layer 95, 174, 176, 177
Interior region 26

J

Juneau 50

K

Kachemak Bay 48
Karluk 59
Kenai 52

Kenai Mountains 48
Kenai Peninsula 48, 52
Kenai River 53
Ketchikan 12, 54, 70
Ketchikan Sneakers 55, 182
King Cove 43
King Salmon 27, 56
Knik Arm 66
Kodiak 58
Kodiak Island 58
Kotzebue 65
Kuskokwim River 38, 60, 61

L

L.L. Bean 176, 186
layering 94, 95, 109, 110
lichens 191
lighting 113
Lite Loft 92

M

magnetic declination 143
Manley Hot Springs 45
maps 142
    DeLorme Mapping 142
    topographic maps 142
Matanuska-Susitna Valley 66
McGrath 26, 60, 61
McKinley National Park 26, 62
McKinley Park 62
Metlakatla 54
midnight sun 31, 36
Moleskin™ 110
monthly snowfall 29
Mountain View Sports Center 187
Mountain Village 39

N

Naknek 57
National Parks 159
natural fabrics 86, 89
Nenana River 62
Ninilchik 52
Nome 26, 64
normal maximum/minimum temperature 28
North Face 78, 187
North Pole 45
Northern Lights 32
Norton Sound 64
nylon taffeta 127

P

packs 145
    Alaskan pack frames 184
    day pack 147
    external frame 144, 145
    fanny pack 147
    Internal frame 145
Palmer 66
Panhandle 25, 54
Paxson 46
Petersburg 77
Point Barrow 36
Polarguard 92, 150, 184
polypropylene 109
polyurethane 127
polyurethane-coated 93, 94, 177
Port Lions 59
precipitation days 28
Primaloft 92, 177
Prince William Sound 74, 75, 154
protective layer 96, 176
Prudhoe Bay 26, 68

Q

Qualofill 92

R

radiation 79, 80
REI 174, 176, 181, 184, 187
renewable natural resources 191
ripstop nylon 127
rule of thirds 112, 113
Russ, Tony 7

S

Sand Point 43
Seldovia 49
semipermeable fabric 130
Seward 75
Seward Peninsula 64
Sierra Trading Post 187, 189
silk 86, 87, 172
Sitka 70
sky conditions 28
sleeping bag 134, 183
   mummy bag 134
   overbag 136
   rectangular bag 134
sleeping cot 138
sleeping pad 137, 184
socks 104, 107, 172
   sock strategy 109
Soldotna 52
Southcentral
   25, 27, 34, 52, 66, 72
Southeast
   25, 51, 54, 55, 71, 76, 104, 149
Southeast region 27
Southwestern 25, 27
Sports Authority 174
spring 27
Sterling 52
stitching awl 150
summer 27
summer solstice 31
Susitna River 72
synthetics 89, 95
   synthetic fabric 90, 91, 127
   synthetic fill material 134
   synthetic insulation 102
   synthetic socks 108

T

Taku winds 51
Talkeetna 72
Talkeetna Mountains 102
tent 128
bivy sack 132
four-season tent 130
freestanding 133
three-season tent 131
tepee 130
The Great Land 101, 121
The Last Frontier 8
The Sportsman's Guide 187
Thermax 90, 95, 109, 173
Thinsulate 92, 102, 180
35mm camera 115
   compact 35mm cameras 117
ThorLo™ socks 108, 174
   ThorLo™ 108
Thorne Bay 54
time zones 31
Togiak 57
Tongass National Forest 54
total precipitation 28
Toughskin™ 110

U

U.S. mail service 123
Unalakleet 65
United States Geological Service 143

V

Valdez 74
Valdez Arm 74
viewpoint 112

W

Wasilla 66, 67
water
   backpacking 162
   purification system 164
   water filters 184
   water needs 161
   water purifiers 184
   water quality 161, 163
water bags 122
water equivalent 14
waterproof fabric 92

waterproofing   105
Western   26
Whittier   75, 154
wind chill   30
WindStopper   90, 175, 177, 180
winter   27
wolves   157
wool   86, 88
Worsterlon   91, 175
Wrangell   76, 149
Wrangell Island   76

Y

Yakutat   51

BIBILIOGRAPHY

Alaska Climate Research Center
903 Koyukuk Dr.
Fairbanks, Ak 99775-7320
907-474-7885
www.wrcc.dri.edu/statclm2.html#ak

Cabela's
One Cabela Drive
Sidney, NE 69160-9555
1-800-237-4444
www.cabelas.com

Western Regional Climate Center
Desert Research Institute
2215 Raggio Parkway
Reno, NV 89512
775-674-7010
www.wrcc.dri.edu

HORN & ANTLER CARVINGS
by TONY RUSS

Native Alaskan, outdoor guide, artist, writer and publisher.

Creations that depict the beauty and majesty of Alaska and her wildlife, captured in materials from the animals themselves.

(Contact Tony at Northern Publishing.)

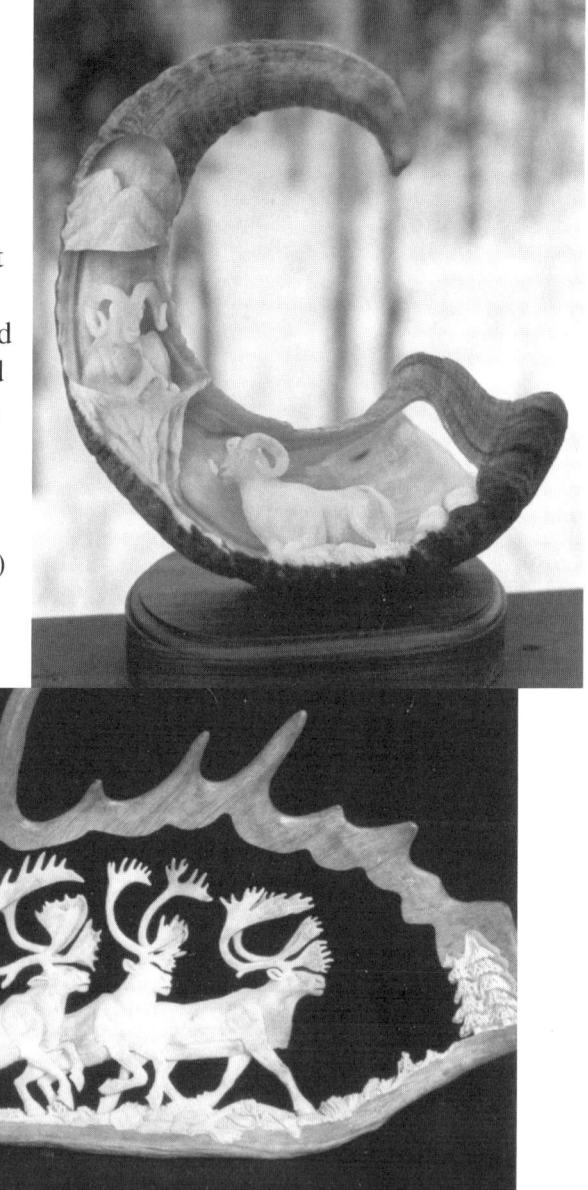

Moose, Caribou, and Sheep horn carvings from your design or mine.

NORTHERN PUBLISHING – ORDER FORM

SHEEP HUNTING IN ALASKA: The Dall Sheep Hunter's Guide, by Tony Russ, 160 pages, 57 photos, $19.95..$_____

THE QUEST FOR DALL SHEEP: A Historic Guide's Memories of Alaskan Hunting, by Jack Wilson, 224 pages, 90 photos, $19.95.................$_____

THE MANUAL FOR SUCCESSFUL HUNTERS: Why 10% of the Hunters Take 90% of the Game, by Tony Russ, 400 pages, 170 photos, 40 illustrations, $24.95...$_____

BOWHUNTING ALASKA, a how-to guide by Ron Swanson, updated in 1997 by Tony Russ, 62 pages, 33 photos, 10 maps, $10.00........................$_____

ALASKA BOWHUNTING RECORDS: Bowhunting records of Alaska's big game animals, by Tony Russ, 128 pages, 23 photos, HARDCOVER; $25.00..............$_____

ALASKA WEAR: The Visitor's Guide to Clothing & Gear, the guide to a comfortable Alaskan visit, by Tony Russ, 200 pages, 150 photos and graphics, $15.95 .... $_____

BOOK TOTAL.................$_____

SHIPPING – $4 per order ....$ 4.00

TOTAL ENCLOSED
(check or money order made
out to Northern Publishing)....$_____

Send books to: _____
_____
_____

Mail Order Form to:
Northern Publishing, P.O. Box 871803, Wasilla, AK 99687-1803